SCRIPTS

SCRIPTS

WRITING FOR RADIO AND TELEVISION

Arthur Asa Berger

SAGE PUBLICATIONS
The International Professional Publishers
Newbury Park   London   New Delhi

For information address:

SAGE Publications, Inc.
2455 Teller Road
Newbury Park, California 91320

SAGE Publications Ltd.
6 Bonhill Street
London EC2A 4PU
United Kingdom

SAGE Publications India Pvt. Ltd.
M-32 Market
Greater Kailash I
New Delhi 110 048 India

Printed in the United States of America

Library of Congress Cataloging-in-Publication Data

Berger, Arthur Asa, 1933–
    Scripts : writing for radio and television / by Arthur Asa Berger.
        p.   cm.
    Includes bibliographical references and index.
    ISBN 0-8039-3761-X. — ISBN 0-8039-3762-8 (pbk.)
    1. Broadcasting—Authorship. I. Title.
PN1991.7.B47 1990
808.2'2—dc20   90-8752
                                                        CIP

FIRST PRINTING, 1990

Sage Production Editor: Astrid Virding

Contents

The radio show demands daily product whether you feel personally up to it or not. Therefore *inspiration* is a moot word.

I usually get to the station by 5 a.m. for a 6 a.m. start. My first action is to throw a piece of paper into the typewriter and set to the task. This is a nonnegotiable situation. Something has to happen. Often I will just start without an idea, typing "Hello, Frank, this is Ronald Reagan calling from the Oval Office." Suddenly, an idea! What if Frank makes a comment that he was looking forward to talking to the chief executive? "Good," says Ron, "I'll get Mommy and put her on the phone." Now I have a direction: Frank convincing Reagan that he's the chief executive and not Nancy.

Sometimes a skit will take direction based on a typo that reads funny, or a newspaper heading stares at you from the desk and gives you direction. The harsh reality of this demanding exercise is that—good or bad—*something has to happen*.

With regard to inspiration, I have developed over the years an ability to remember those sketchy but valuable flashes of brilliance—or so we think—that hit you any time of day or night. Sometimes I will use the afternoon to then write and edit something without the strict time constraints of the morning. That's a luxury.

I have come to the salty, unromantic conclusion that writing is tough, inspired or not. But gritty determination and a developed self-discipline will get words onto paper, or, in this case, into some word processor. And I love to write. Need I say more?

—Mike Cleary on getting words onto paper
(personal correspondence with Arthur Berger, August 31, 1989)

Preface

This book is about writing scripts.

It deals with styles and comedy writing and the basic formats used in radio and television scripts for commercials, features, news, documentaries, public service announcements, editorials, reviews, and teleplays. While *Scripts* was designed specifically for radio and television writing courses, it can be used in any course in which writing is important.

Where is it ordained that students must always write essays? I've noticed that many of my students have a remarkable flair for writing dialogue and enjoy writing scripts. Why don't we take advantage of this and ask them to try their hand at writing scripts in courses other than those dealing with writing for the broadcast media?

Aside from the tactical reasons for encouraging scriptwriting in such courses (English, history, American studies, sociology—one might go on and on), there are good pedagogical and intellectual ones as well. Scripts rely upon the power of dialogue, a subject that now is of great interest to literary scholars. The Russian literary theorist M. M. Bakhtin, who some consider one of the most important thinkers of the twentieth century, has discussed the power of dialogue in a number of his works. A book of his essays is called, fittingly, *The Dialogical Imagination*. Dialogue may seem simple but the way it functions is, it turns out, rather complex.

Why not switch, from time to time, from the essentially "monologic" voice, found in essays, to scripts and a dialogic one? Students spend a good deal of their time watching stories (full of dialogue) that they find interesting and exciting. We should capitalize on this. Instead of always requiring students to write an essay or a term paper on a subject, why not ask them, occasionally, to write a documentary? Students might also find it stimulating to be asked to do an anniversary feature on some person or event of historic significance, or create a "public interest" commercial to deal with some social issue. The possibilities are endless.

In order to keep *Scripts* relatively short, I have written it in a schematic manner in places. This imposes some burdens on my readers, I realize, but I don't think they are too oppressive. *Scripts* also contains a number of assignments and exercises I've used in class that my students have found interesting and useful, which I offer as suggestions or as possible ways to use the material covered in each chapter.

The writing-across-the-curriculum movement has made great progress in getting instructors, in all disciplines, to include journal writing and other kinds of writing in their courses. *Scripts* should be seen as a further contribution to this movement, extending the range of writing opportunities offered to students.

I've started each chapter off with a quotation that demonstrates a different style of writing. The quotations don't necessarily have anything to do with the subjects of the chapters they precede, though in some cases they do. I think the passages are interesting and, in many cases, remarkable. Some of the passages are very famous and others are ones not many people are familiar with. I hope they will suggest the possibilities available to writers and help widen stylistic horizons.

Acknowledgments

I would like to thank Mitch Allen, who suggested I write *Scripts*, and Ann West, my editor, who did a wonderful job of encouraging me and shepherding me through the production of the book. I would also like to express my appreciation to a number of other people who have helped me, one way or another, with the book: Jane Morrison, Len Schlosser, Anna Geddes, John Hewitt, Herb Kaplan, Nate Shoehalter, Russ Johnson, Lans Hays, Joan Van Tassel, Corless Smith, Stuart Hyde, Bob Johnson (of Johnson and Joyce Advertising), Bruce Mowery and Tracy Gifford (of Apple Computer Company), the Radio Advertising Bureau, Ray Barrett (of KCBS Radio in San Francisco), the Coyote Point Museum, Carolyn Wean (of KPIX-TV in San Francisco), and my students in the Broadcast Communication Arts Department, who have made teaching my course on writing for radio and television both a challenge and a joy. Also I would like to thank Mary Beth DeHainaut, Judy Selhorst, and Astrid Virding for bringing this book to press. Finally, my wife, Phyllis, gave me a great deal of moral support while I worked on the book.

The Father: But don't you see that the whole trouble lies here. In words, words. Each one of us has within him a whole world of things, each man of us his own special world. And how can we ever come to an understanding if I put in the words I utter the sense and value of things as I see them; while you who listen to me must inevitably translate them according to the conception of things each one of you has within himself. We think we understand each other, but we never really do. . . .

—Luigi Pirandello, *Six Characters in Search of an Author*
(1952, p. 224)

Introduction

It was while dining on salt-roasted prawns and stuffed bean curd at the Heavenly Ocean restaurant in San Francisco that I decided to write this book. I was having lunch with an editor—one of the many side benefits of being a writer is that editors take you to lunch—and we were talking about books I might write. After a while I happened to say something about the writing courses I'd been teaching. "I've been teaching broadcast writing a good deal," I said. "I've got a number of ideas about how to teach it and have had a lot of fun in my classes. I think I'd like to write a book called 'Six Formats in Search of an Author,' taking off on the title of Pirandello's play."

He snapped his fingers and said, "That's it."

When that happened I realized that I had, somehow, found the project I was looking for. The rest is history . . . and an incredible amount of hard work. But also great pleasure, for I really love to write.

How is this book different from all other books that deal with writing for broadcasting? *Scripts* is a book that will teach you how to write some of the basic kinds of scripts used in radio and television broadcasting. In that respect, it is like any number of other books. But it is different in that it takes a somewhat unique approach to writing and it has a good deal of original material on comedy writing.

Scriptwriting Is Fun

Why is it that when we are young we love to draw pictures and write stories, but that when we get older we lose the desire to do either? I don't know the answer to these questions, but it must have something to do with the education process and with anxieties we develop about making mistakes in our writing and revealing things about ourselves through our writing.

As a result of taking numerous composition courses and being required to write essays and term papers in other courses, many of my students come into broadcast writing courses with a considerable amount of apprehension. (There is reason for this, too, I might add—because many students have not been taught the essentials of grammar.) Fortunately, writing scripts is different from writing expository prose. Most of the formats we will be dealing with involve dialogue and an informal, conversational style of writing.

In scripts, characters talk in sentence fragments—because that's the way we usually talk when we converse. And script-writers use sound as well as music, narration, and, in the case of television, visual images in their scripts. Scriptwriting is much more of a right-side-of-the-brain activity than essay writing. In scripts there is a premium on being imaginative, inventive, lively, and entertaining, not that these qualities are lacking in good essays. It is just that scriptwriting seems to make being creative easier—because it generally involves inventing characters and situations—and requires one to be imaginative.

Scripts deals with some of the most fundamental genres for radio and television: public service announcements, commercials, features, teleplays, reviews, editorials, news, and documentaries. And it provides examples of each of these genres, as well—generally material that has actually been broadcast. So you can see how the professionals do things.

Styles of Writing

The book begins with a chapter on styles of writing. We tend to lose sight of the fact that there are a variety of ways we can write something. We can adopt any one of numerous styles, depending upon the audience we wish to reach and the reasons we are writing. Consider commercials, for example. We sometimes have a product that will appeal to an "upscale" market rather than a "downscale" one. Then, we have to write a commercial according to our understanding of what "upscale" people are like—what motivates them, what interests them, what turns them on and off.

My point is, then, that we never just write. We always write with our readers, listeners, or viewers in mind—whether we are writing a letter, essay, term paper, or script. The purpose of the chapter on styles is to open up a broad spectrum of possibilities for my readers and help them appreciate the different "voices" they can adopt when they write.

Curiously enough, we are continually exposed to different styles of writing, but we generally don't pay much attention to them. Our interest in style tends to be focused on fashion, not writing. I think style is so important that I start with it and mention it frequently. And I provide a chart with many different styles that you can use, depending upon the circumstances.

Formats

Next comes a brief discussion of the script formats we use when writing for radio and television. *There are no universally accepted formats,* but I think you will find that my formatting suggestions make good sense. I will use the split-page format for both radio and television nonfiction scripts and offer some examples of scripts that have been used for various radio and television productions. The format for teleplay scripts is different and is discussed in the chapter dealing with them.

A format is like a guide for driving; it doesn't matter too much what the rules are as long as everyone knows them, understands them, and obeys them.

Comedy Writing

I have been writing about humor for many years and have actually taught courses devoted entirely to comedy writing.

"What's that?" you say. "Teaching comedy writing? How can you *teach* people to be funny?"

The answer is, of course, you can't. That is, you can't take people without any sense of humor, or with an undeveloped sense of humor, and teach them how to be funny. But you can take people with well-developed comedic sensibilities and teach them a number of methods that they can use to write good comedy.

I have developed a methodology for teaching comedy writing that works. I say this because many of my students, after a bit of coaching and after I've taught them something about what makes people laugh, have written some wonderful, extremely funny, short scripts. It might be more accurate to say that I don't teach people how to be funny but, instead, teach them techniques that enable them to use their gifts to produce some really excellent humorous material.

Journals

I have kept a journal since 1954 and believe that it is my journals that have been instrumental in my becoming a writer. ("Aha!" says the critic. "So you admit it. Your books are all really autobiographies, in one form or another.") After 35 years of writing journals I have some rather strong ideas on how journals should be kept and I will offer these as suggestions for keeping journals. I make a distinction, I might add, between journals (which deal with ideas and such things) and diaries (which are very personal).

I make my writing students keep journals and often ask them to write in their journals during class periods—a trick I picked up from a very valuable workshop I took on writing across the curriculum. I will show some examples from my journals, to show how I do it. I would say that journal keeping is the single most important thing a writer can do, for by having a journal, fugitive thoughts, ideas, and notions that come to mind and are usually forgotten can be saved and worked upon.

Radio and Television Genres

I devote a number of chapters to the major genres of radio and television. I start with commercials, move on to radio features, and then deal with television documentaries and news. The next three chapters deal with genres that are closer to standard prose essays—public service announcements, editorials, and reviews. I conclude the section on genres with a chapter on writing dramas for television. In each chapter I offer examples of scripts, discuss important things to keep in mind (relative to each genre), and suggest various assignments and classroom activities that I have found useful and my students have found entertaining.

Common Writing Errors

I will offer a short chapter that focuses on a number of the most common errors people make when they write. My theory is that if I can teach people how to avoid a small number of very basic errors, what we might call in legal jargon "repeat offenders," I can help them improve their writing a great deal.

I will also say something about what I consider to be "good" writing—writing that has detail and character and generates interest in readers. I also make some suggestions about revising, especially for writers who use word processors. I argue that corrections should be made on hard copy rather than at the video screen. There are a couple of reasons for this: It helps avoid eyestrain and it seems to be more effective.

Know the Author

I've published 16 books and numerous articles on such topics as pop culture, comics, television, film, and the media. I always was torn, when I was a kid, between my love of writing and my love of drawing. I solved the problem by becoming a writer who illustrates his own books (and books and articles by many others, I should add). I've also studied creative writing. I attended the famous workshop for writers at the University of Iowa (while I was working on my M.A. in journalism) and studied with a fabulous writer and person, Marguerite Young. I also had the privilege of studying creative writing with one of America's greatest writers, Allen Tate, when he taught at the University of Minnesota (where I was working on my Ph.D. in American studies).

After graduating from the University of Iowa I was drafted and spent two years writing public relations material for the U.S. Army in Washington, D.C. I also wrote high school sports for the *Washington Post* during this period, which may explain my interest in things like football and wrestling.

Since graduating from the University of Minnesota in 1965, I've been writing nonstop, so it seems, on a wide variety of subjects, most of which are connected with media and popular culture. I recently published a book on visual communication that I enjoyed writing and that is full of my illustrations.

I have something of a reputation among communication scholars (deservedly, no doubt) as being a bit of comedian, prankster, and clown, and, worst of all, for not being serious about academia or scholarship—or myself. I have been known to make terrible puns (as well as some really good ones), to take questionable ideas and play around with them, to write offbeat and perhaps even eccentric essays and books. In certain respects, relating to my ideas (probably my fondness for Freudian thought) and style of writing and lecturing, I find myself an outsider. In some respects, it is a good position to be in, because I have a lot of freedom.

As an editor said to me recently, "If we could just give you a little twist, Arthur, so your stuff was more conventional . . ." Then she picked up her hands and made a brief twisting motion in the air. She was trying to figure out how to harness my energy and imagination (or should I say what she considered to be my "wildness") into a project that would appeal to my peers—the professors who, after all, have to adopt any textbooks I write and their students who, it is hoped, will read my books.

I don't think you will find this book particularly zany or offbeat, though I do think it is different from other writing books that are available. I have intentionally written in an informal, perhaps even breezy, style. I have done this because I want to do everything I can to get you to read it; I am, with my style, sugarcoating the didactic pill, which is another way of saying I am making things "taste good" that might not be, if prepared in another manner, too palatable.

I do have a "serious" style that I use in certain cases, but I do not think it would be useful to write in this manner here.

I sometimes describe my teaching method (and stance in general) as being "Zenlike." The ancient Zen teachers, it turns out, took on the persona or "mask" of clowns when they taught and indulged in horseplay, puns, non sequiturs, jokes, pranks, irrationality, and that kind of thing. If you find this kind of thing in the book you will have to decide whether it is a rational (and calculated) decision on my part or, instead, a rationalization by someone who can't resist a play on words or a crazy idea.

My Hopes for You

I hope you will find this book useful (in that it teaches you something about writing) and entertaining (in that it provides you with some ideas to consider and techniques that will help you with your writing). Large numbers of people, who don't have to worry about teachers grading them down for misplaced modifiers or faulty pronoun reference, love to write. The number of people writing for pleasure—knocking out scripts, articles, mysteries, science fiction stories, novels, screenplays, and books on every subject imaginable and some that are unimaginable—is legion. These people would give anything to be able to make a living as writers.

I would be pleased if *Scripts* helps you to conquer your fears of writing and enables some of you to try your luck at becoming professional writers. Somebody has to write all the commercials, news stories, dramas, sitcoms, documentaries, and comedy shows we hear on the radio and see on television. Why not you?

PART I

Prescriptions

Suddenly, through the churning white, I saw the girl running away from me, toward the ice. I tried to shout, "Stop! Come back!" but the polar air corroded my throat, my voice was whirled away by the wind. Snow powder blowing round me like mist, I ran after her. I could hardly see her, hardly see out of my eyes: I had to pause, painfully wipe away the crystals of ice forming on my eyeballs, before I could continue. The murderous wind kept hurling me back, the snow heaped up white hills that fumed like volcanoes, blinding me again with white smoke. In the awful dead cold I lurched on, reaching her somehow at last, clutched her with numbed hands. . . . A mirage-like arctic splendour towered all around, a weird, unearthly architecture of ice. Huge ice-battlements, rainbow turrets and pinnacles, filled the sky, lit from within by frigid mineral fires. We were trapped by those encircling walls, a ring of ghostly executioners, advancing slowly, inexorably, to destroy us. I could not move, could not think. The executioner's breath paralysed, dulled the brain. I felt the fatal chill of the ice touch me, heard its thunder, saw it split by dazzling emerald fissures. Far overhead the iceberg-glittering heights boomed and shuddered, about to fall.

—Anna Kavan, *Ice* (1973, p. 120)

1

Style

There is no writing without style. It is just that some writing—perhaps most writing—is done in a style that is so dull and ordinary that we lose sight of the fact that it has a style. Let me offer an analogy that might be useful. At one time, some social thinkers held that there were people who didn't have "culture." These thinkers usually defined *culture* as involving the elite arts—classical music, the opera, poetry, so-called great literature—as well as certain forms of social organization and literacy. But many people in the world don't have our elite arts or literacy. That doesn't mean they don't have culture.

We now realize that all humans have culture, for it is culture that makes us humans. In the same vein, every writer has a style of writing. It is just that most people don't write particularly well, so we tend to overlook their style of writing. We cannot write without style, but we can write in a style so bland and ordinary that our writing *seems* styleless.

This leads to the question—what is style?

Style usually involves some form of expression—involving such matters as the way we comb (or style) our hair, the clothes we wear, the way we live (our life-style), and the way we write. We often make a distinction between fashion, which involves changes in styles, and style itself, which involves some kind of distinctiveness, uniqueness, and personality in the ways we express ourselves.

For our purposes, it is useful to think of style as involving a way of writing that is personal, distinctive, and unique, to the extent that we are able to achieve this. It is not easily done. I would describe this as "personal style." The great writers have their own styles and their work is immediately recognizable. I am talking here about the way they use language and, in the case of fiction, about the characters and plots they create.

21

Think of Hemingway. His style, which is remarkably simple (on the face of it) is highly distinctive. So much so, as a matter of fact, that Hemingway is frequently parodied and there is an annual contest in which the best ridiculous imitation of Hemingway is given a prize. It may be that the sign of a personal style is the degree to which it can be parodied and made fun of.

Good Writing and Poor Writing

How do we differentiate between a good style of writing and a poor style of writing? It's hard to say, because writing is an art and there are no hard-and-fast rules that everyone recognizes about what is good and what is bad. In the case of literature, for example, we find that tastes change, and our estimates of who is good and bad (or important and minor) change rapidly over the years.

In the case of ordinary writing, however, it is possible to make some generalizations that many people would find reasonable.

Good Writing	Poor Writing
grammatically correct	grammatically incorrect
fluid, coherent	choppy, fragmented
imaginative	dull, prosaic
personality	undistinctive
interesting ideas	highly conventional ideas
figurative language	simplistic structure
easy to read	hard to read

Good writing is grammatically correct; writing that is not correct causes readers or listeners all kinds of problems because it is hard to figure out what the writer is trying to say. But one can write correctly without being a good writer. That is, grammatical correctness is a necessary but not sufficient characteristic of good writing.

What really counts, I suggest, is the degree to which writers manifest their personalities, give their work spirit, vitality, and energy. The reason we don't find these qualities in most writing is that most people have to work so hard expressing themselves in even the simplest manner that they don't have time or energy left for putting character and personality into their writing. This is because they haven't been taught correctly, probably don't read very much (reading generally correlates with good writing), and don't write very often. You can't learn to play the piano well without practicing and you can't learn to write well without doing a good deal of writing.

Many extremely intelligent people write poorly, because our educational system has let them down. You can't write well if you don't keep at it and if you don't have proper guidance—unless you are extremely dedicated and find a way, somehow, to teach yourself.

Some students have the silly idea that an excessively formal style is the key to good writing. And so they write papers in a labored manner and perpetrate such atrocities as "It is the opinion of this author that" instead of "I think." They get this notion from reading some scholarly articles and books, which are written in a very formal manner.

In broadcast writing, fortunately, we don't have to worry about this—though students often forget about writing in a conversational style and lapse into an excessively formal style.

Many writers make a distinction between form and content. What I have been calling "style" would fall under form; I would argue, however, that form and content are not separate, but are really tied together. How you write affects what you write; style has an impact on content and is really part of it, just as content can be seen as part of form.

Technical Devices

There is also the matter of what I could call "technical devices" that can be adopted to give one's written work a bit of character. When we write we can use a number of different devices to give our writing color and interest. Let me list some of them:

(1) *Alliteration.* Here we start a number of words with the same sound. This shows we have a certain command over

language and like to play around with it. Alliteration also has a dramatic effect.

(2) *Repetition.* This device involves consciously repeating some word or phrase over and over for dramatic impact. Repetition by itself is boring, but in certain situations it can be very effective.

(3) *Balance.* We use balance to give certain parts of our writing a kind of structure and symmetry. If all of our writing were balanced it would be rather tedious, but in some places it is very effective—especially when we are comparing things or dealing with ideas.

(4) *Description.* In radio scripts we use description to give our listeners a visual picture of some kind. Radio has been described as the "theater of the mind" because of the power of our imaginations to "see" things, in our own way, that have been described to us.

(5) *Figurative language.* We use metaphors (comparisons in which we equate one thing with another) and similes (comparisons in which we describe one thing as being like or as another) to give our writing richness. Seeing one thing in terms of another is a tool for generating insight and understanding in our readers or listeners. "Love *is* a game" is a metaphor. "Love is *like* a game" is a simile. It is a weaker kind of comparison.

We often write figuratively without realizing we are doing so. Consider the following:

The ship glided through the water.
The ship cut through the water.
The ship raced through the water.
The ship knifed through the water.
The ship danced through the water.

In each of these cases we are using verbs metaphorically: gliding (like a plane or glider), cutting (like a knife), racing (as in a race), knifing (like a knife), and dancing (like a dancer). Each of these verbs suggest something slightly different about how the ship is moving through the water.

The Exact Word

This leads to an important insight: *Every word we use has an impact, conveying a particular meaning or impression.* When we write, then, especially when we write for the ear, we must be extremely careful about the language we use. A change in one word, the substitution of one word for another, can have a big impact on the way we interpret what is written or said.

The French have a wonderful expression, *le mot juste,* which means "the right word" or "the exact word." In the discussion of verbs above, I suggested that different verbs convey different impressions and senses of things. We have to find the "exact" word to get our ideas across and give our listeners the correct impression. This is where revising becomes important.

After we have roughed in a first draft of a script, and gotten our ideas across, we have to revise the draft and polish it up. This is where the process of finding the exact word comes into play, for there is a world of difference between having an acceptable word and having the exact word in the script. Writing is, to a great extent, the art of conveying impressions by the use of language, so it is only natural that finding the exact word is extremely important.

Public Writing Style

Up to this point I have been discussing writing styles in terms of individuals, and the way individuals write. I have suggested that there is no such thing as writing without style and that the seeming "stylelessness" of much of the writing that we see is really a kind of style, or perhaps an antistyle, in that it is undistinctive and perhaps even anonymous. The writing frequently is not grammatically correct.

Let me offer an analogy that might be useful here. Think of a dancing school. Some people are busy learning the steps and it is a great effort for them just to do the steps. Others have mastered the steps and are concerned with developing distinctive and exciting ways of dancing, and are dancing with "flair."

I will carry the dancing analogy a step or two further. Although we can move around as we wish when dancing to certain kinds of music, such as rock, there are other dances that have definite steps to them—the waltz, the samba, the rumba, the cha-cha-cha, and so on. The best dancers do the correct steps, yet go beyond them. In the same light, there are what might be called public or conventional writing styles that we often adopt in certain situations.

We come across these styles all the time, but seldom pay any attention to them. (This is because most of us are not writers and do not concern ourselves very much with writing and matters such as style.) We may even use these public styles from time to time. Let me offer an example. In the good old days (that's just a year or so ago), before the development of fax machines, people found it necessary to send telegrams. Because one pays for every word in a telegram, what we might describe as a "telegraphic" style of writing developed—in which we reduced our messages to the basic elements.

Instead of writing "I will be arriving Sunday evening at 8:30 p.m. on Flight 237. Please meet me at the arrival gate. I look forward to seeing you. Sincerely, John Q. Public," we would write something like this: "Arrive Sunday 8:30 p.m. Stop. Meet arrival gate. Stop. John Q. Public. Stop."

Examples of Writing Styles

There are, it turns out, dozens of these public or conventional writing styles that we can adopt, depending upon our needs and the audience we are trying to reach. All of these styles are part of our general knowledge and can be very useful from time to time. We can employ one or more of them in certain circumstances when we wish to give our listeners an impression of one kind or another. Below is a list of a number of the most common styles of writing:

Writing Styles

bureaucratic	telegraphic	poetic/lyrical	college bulletin
slang	discursive	flowery	intellectual
jargon	legalistic	journalistic	exclamatory

technocratic	mystical	ideological	witty
biblical	textbookish	metaphoric	comic-stripish
rap style	primer style	absurdist	sportswriterish
dialects	paradoxical	advertising	psychotic
blurb	passive voice	Latinate	operatic
philosophical	insults	haiku	pig latin

I assume we are all familiar with most of the styles listed above. But let me characterize some of them to make sure readers understand what I'm talking about. I am simplifying matters considerably, but I think you'll get a sense of what each of these styles is like.

Style	Characteristics
bureaucratic	informal, impersonal, convoluted
poetic/lyrical	flowery language, romantic
primer style	short, choppy sentences; for 5-year-olds
psychotic	internal dialogue, paranoid (or other)
legalistic	party of the first part, contractual
paradoxical	full of purposely stated contradictions
witty	with puns and word play
journalistic	adopts who/what/where/when/why formula
ideological	full of right-/left-wing terms, clichés
advertising	tries to persuade, sell product/service/idea
metaphorical	uses similes and metaphors whenever possible
philosophical	very abstract, long sentences, abstruse
biblical	archaic language, well-known characters used
intellectual	hypercomplex, pretentious, obscure
technocratic	scientific jargon about devices and processes
dialects	Russian, Italian, French, German
rap	rhyming verse with a beat

Raymond Queneau: Exercises in Style

There is a wonderful book by a French writer, Raymond Queneau, called *Exercises in Style* (1981) (English translation), that writers interested in style might wish to consult. In this remarkable book Queneau offers a virtuoso display of stylistic writing. He tells a very simple little story, 15 lines long, that serves as the first chapter of the book. Then he retells the same story, using different styles, 60 or 70 different ways. What he shows is that there is no *one* way to write a story—or anything else; there is, in fact, a huge number of different ways we can write something.

Let me quote a few passages from this book. The story involves a young man with a felt hat (with a cord instead of a ribbon for a hatband) who takes an "S" bus. He accuses a fellow passenger of jostling him, eventually finds a seat and sits down, and is seen two hours later talking to a friend, who tells him he should get an extra button put on his overcoat.

What follows are short portions from a few of Queneau's exercises in style.

Official Letter Style
I beg to advise you of the following facts of which I happened to be the equally impartial and horrified witness. Today, at roughly twelve noon, I was present on the platform of a bus which was proceeding up the rue de Courcelles. . . . (p. 21)

Cross-Examination Style
—At what time did the 12:23 p.m. S-line bus proceeding in the direction of the Porte de Champerret arrive on that day?

—At 12:38 p.m.

—Were there many people on the aforesaid S bus?

—Bags of 'em. (p. 27)

Dream
I had the impression that everything was misty and nacreous around me, with multifarious and indistinct apparitions, amongst whom however was one figure that stood out fairly clearly which was that of a young man whose too-long neck. . . . (p. 54)

Double Entry
Towards the middle of the day and at midday I happened to be on and got on to the platform and balcony at the back of an S-line and of a Contrescarpe-Champeret bus and passenger transport. . . . (p. 90)

I think you can see what Queneau is up to. What Queneau shows, in his amusing and brilliantly conceived book, is how many different ways we can write something. Above I have offered my list of styles we might adopt as a way of helping writers develop different ways of writing—regardless of the medium they are writing for, or the genre of work they are writing.

More Examples of Styles

College Bulletin. Here is an example of what I would call the college catalog "course description" style of writing:

> *Philosophy 25: The Best Things in Life*
> Robert Nozick
>   A philosophical examination of the nature and value of those things deemed best, such as friendship, love, intellectual under-standing, sensual pleasure, achievement, adventure, play, luxury, fame, power, enlightenment, and ice cream.

This example comes from a Harvard University catalog of courses of instruction and describes a course taught by one of the most eminent philosophers of the present day.

Philosophical. Here is a quotation from one of the philosophical classics, Immanuel Kant's *Groundwork of the Metaphysic Morals*:

> Since the universality of the law governing the production of effects constitutes what is properly called *nature* in its most general sense (nature as regards form)—that is, the existence of things so far as determined by universal laws—the universal imperative of duty may also run as follows: "*Act as if the maxim of your action were to become through your will a universal law of nature.*"

This passage, incidentally, expresses one of Kant's classic notions, that of the categorical imperative, an idea that has been one of the foundations of Western theories of ethics.

Academic. This style is found in scholarly books and journals and is characterized by a very high level of abstraction, by the use of a specialized language, and by reference to ideas and works with which readers are probably familiar. In the passage that follows, from sociologist Todd Gitlin, we also find ideological writing, as Gitlin is generally identified as being on the political left. The quote is from an article titled "Television's Screens: Hegemony in Transition" (1987):

> These tensions within hegemonic ideology render it vulnerable to the demands of insurgent groups and to cultural change in general. Insurgencies press upon the hegemonic whole in the name of one of its components—against the demands of others. *And popular culture is one crucial institution where the rival claims of ideology are sometimes pressed forward, sometimes reconciled in imaginative form.* Popular culture absorbs oppositional ideology, adapts it to the contours of the core hegemonic principle, and domesticates it; at the same time, popular culture is a realm for the expression of forms of resistance and oppositional ideology. (p. 242)

Some readers may find this passage difficult, but we must remember that Gitlin is dealing with a very complicated subject and is writing, primarily, for an audience that is interested in his ideas and familiar with this style of writing. If you look at his style of writing, aside from his use of some technical terms (and he defines *hegemony* earlier in the essay), the writing is rather simple and straightforward and not full of hypersyllabic Latinate word constructions or complicated sentence structures.

These selections offer, I believe, good examples of some of the different styles of writing that are available to us. We have to consider our audiences when we evaluate writing, and when we decide which styles to use. Primer-style writing ("Look, John. See the dog. The dog's name is Spot. Run, Spot.") is inappropriate for adults but perfectly appropriate for young children with limited vocabularies who are learning how to read.

Revising: Postproduction Word Work

Woody Allen has said that he usually revises his work five or six times, and describes himself as a "compulsive rewriter."

In a film about him, *Woody Allen*, he points out that the hard part is getting an original idea and getting a first draft down. After that, he keeps on revising and rewriting until he gets things exactly the way he wants them.

That's why I suggest that writing is very much like editing television programs—it is the postproduction work that is crucial, that turns a rough draft into a finished and polished work. In order to have time to revise, you must get a rough draft of your script done as soon as you can, leave a bit of time so you can get some distance from the script, and then have enough time to work on the script (or whatever piece of writing you are involved with).

Allen has said that he never writes for more than a few hours a day. The secret of being productive, he suggests, is getting to the typewriter (or word processor) *regularly*. This means that writers must develop a certain amount of discipline: They must write regularly and they must allow themselves a good deal of time to rewrite and revise their work. One of the most important aspects of writing, then, is learning how to manage your time.

Media, Genres, and Styles

I make distinctions among media, popular art forms (or genres), and styles. I have already discussed the various styles we might adopt when we write. In the lists below, I differentiate between the media and the genres carried in the media:

Media	*Popular Art Forms Found in the Media*	
radio	commercials	sports
television	documentaries	action-adventure
newspapers	editorials	programs
magazines	public service	game shows
books	announcements	soap operas
records	news	spectacles
film	reviews	situation comedies
	science fiction	variety shows

A medium is a means of carrying various popular art forms or genres. In the electronic media, these genres are commonly known as shows or programs. The electronic media not only carry programs but also affect the programs they carry.

In this book, the focus is on writing for radio and television, the broadcasting media, and on some of the most important genres they carry. But once you learn how to write a script for a radio feature, for example, there is nothing to prevent you from trying your hand at some other genre for some other medium. If you can write well, you can learn the relatively straightforward script formats for each medium and the conventions for each genre.

Exercises

1. Here are some elements for a story:

A tall young man carrying a green backpack boards a bus. He brushes against a little old lady and almost knocks her over. He excuses himself. After three stops he finds an empty seat. After three more stops he gets off the bus. He is seen, shortly after, talking with a young woman with long blonde hair.

Tell this story in any three of the following styles:

internal dialogue (paranoid)	metaphoric
rap	ideological
sportswriter	telegraphic
primer	legalistic
biblical	discursive

2. Rewrite one version of the story three or four different times and see how the last version compares with the first one.

3. Analyze an essay or story from some book or magazine. Discuss the selection's style, or the different styles used in it. What's good about it? What don't you like about it? Try your hand at rewriting it.

4. How would you describe or characterize your style of writing? Be specific. Then find an example of your writing and analyze it. What changes would you like to make in the way you write? How do you intend to make these changes?

5. In groups of three, try the genre writing exercise described in Exhibit 1.1.

Exhibit 1.1: Genre Writing

We can make a distinction between a medium (plural is *media*) such as film or television and the kinds of programs it carries/transmits, namely, genres. Some of the more popular television genres are as follows:

horror	commercials
science fiction	religious
spy fiction	soap opera
tough-guy detective	talk show
intellectual detective	sports show
news	situation comedy

In this exercise, first determine the basic conventions in each genre. Genres are very formulaic and have certain traits that distinguish them from other genres.

location for story
kinds of characters involved (heroes, villains, etc.)
time (when the story is taking place)
basic conventions of the plot (what happens)
style of language used (tone, mood, etc.)
anything else you can think of

Here are the elements of the story. You can manipulate these elements any way you wish, depending upon the requirements of the genres you choose. Write two short radio plays, using the proper format with dialogue, music, sound effects, and so on.

(1) Beautiful young woman, Virginia, is reading a book.

(2) Door opens and handsome young man, Elmer, enters.

(3) Virginia gets up. They embrace. Are interrupted by phone.

(4) Virginia answers. Has a subdued conversation. She says something to Elmer, then takes an attaché case and leaves.

(5) She drives to the university and has an espresso in the Student Union. While she is sitting there, a man with gray hair comes over and says something to her. He sits down. She opens her attaché case and shows him a piece of paper.

(6) She glances at her watch. She gets up, runs out of the room, and is seen entering a large building, where she gets lost in a crowd of students.

(7) Your conclusion to the story.

Exhibit 1.2: Descriptive Writing

Tolstoy makes the familiar seem strange by not naming the familiar object. He describes an object as if he were seeing it for the first time, an event as if it were happening for the first time. For example, in "Shame" Tolstoy "defamiliarizes" the idea of flogging in this way: "to strip people who have broken the law, to hurl them to the floor, and to rap on their bottoms with switches," and, after a few lines, "to lash about on the naked buttocks." (Victor Shklovsky, "Art as Technique")

In this exercise, we will avoid naming people, things, and events to the extent possible, and rely, instead, on descriptions.

Write a monologue in which a person describes his or her morning. This involves the following elements:

(1) Being wakened by an alarm clock or clock radio at 7:30 a.m.
(2) Taking a shower, brushing teeth, etc.
(3) Getting dressed—wearing shorts and a T-shirt.
(4) Having breakfast with family. Mother cooks. Meal is orange juice, oatmeal with hot milk, bacon and eggs, toast and strawberry jam, coffee, and cream.
(5) Father has breakfast, with a brother (14) and sister (19).
(6) Take bus to school and go to room 40 for writing class.
(7) A professor comes in and talks about writing.

Remember: Avoid naming things/events/people to the extent possible, but don't go overboard and try to describe everything and not use any names. This is impossible.

6. In groups of three, try the descriptive writing exercise described in Exhibit 1.2.

BUDDY: Well, Dad, I never had a chance to try anything else. I had two years of college, then the Army, and then right into business. Maybe it's not the right field for me.

FATHER: Not the right field? *(He addresses an imaginary listener in right center chair)* I give the boy the biggest artificial fruit manufacturing house in the East, he tells me *not the right field.* Ha!

(He sits right center chair)

BUDDY: I don't know if I've got any talent . . . but . . . I've always toyed with the idea of becoming a writer.

FATHER: A writer? What kind of writer? Letters? *(He holds up letter)* Letters you write beautiful. I don't know who's going to buy them, but they're terrific.

BUDDY: But supposing I'm good? I'm not even getting a chance to find out. Supposing I could write plays . . . for television or for theater?

FATHER: Plays can close. *(Crossing to him)* Television you turn off. Wax fruit lays in the bowl till you're a hundred.

—Neil Simon, *Come Blow Your Horn*

2

Formats

In this chapter I will deal with the basic formats used in preparing scripts for radio and television programming. I am using the term *format* to mean the way a script looks, the conventions we will be adopting in writing the script. Actually, there are no universally agreed-upon script formats, but there are certain ways of designing scripts that most writers use (with minor variations here and there).

Before I discuss these formats, however, I would like to say something about writing for the ear. This is because when we write our scripts we must write for the ear and this is somewhat different from the kind of writing we do when we write essays or term papers, which are written primarily for the eye.

Writing for the Ear

Keep It Simple. This is the cardinal rule. Avoid long, complex, convoluted sentences and constructions that will confuse listeners. This doesn't mean you have to write in a simpleminded manner (close to what I described earlier as primer-style writing). It does mean that you have to make things as easy as you can for your listeners. Remember, they cannot reread what you have written. They have but one chance to "catch" what you say, so make the most of it.

Be Mindful of Flow. Make sure that your script has good continuity and moves from one point to the next in a fluid manner. You have to help your listeners by making sure your script is logically organized and by using transitions that guide them along the way and help them make sense of things. In the chart below, I've listed some of the most common transitions and shown how they function. These transitions are important in all writing, I might add, not just in scripts.

Offering Examples	*Conclusions Reached*	*Argument Continues*
for example	therefore	furthermore
for instance	thus	in addition
to show this	we find, then	to continue
as an illustration	to sum up	moreover
Contrasting Ideas	*Causes*	*Effects*
but	because	therefore
on the other hand	this leads to	as a result
in contrast	since	accordingly
nevertheless		the consequence is
Sequence	*Time Relation*	*Meaning*
first	before	this means
next	after	we find, then
furthermore	meanwhile	this suggests
to begin with	at the same time	this implies

These transitions, as you can see, help listeners make sense of what they have learned and anticipate what is coming. Transitions establish the logical structure of scripts. This does not mean they have to be used in every instance or in a mechanical manner, but you must use enough of them to help your listeners follow you—whether you are writing a documentary, a commercial, or an editorial.

Write in a Lively Manner. Try to inject an appropriate amount of vitality, personality, and spirit into your script. You can do this by writing in the active voice, by using the right adjectives and adverbs, and by developing some kind of a personal style (taking advantage of the various styles, described in the previous chapter, that are available to you). Your script should not read like a term paper that is being performed on the air. This does not mean you cannot deal with serious and important subjects or that you always have to write in a witty, breezy style. Your style must be appropriate to your subject matter, but the writing should be lively and have authority to it.

Sound Natural. You do this by using language that is not stilted or overly formal and by adopting a *conversational* style of writing. When people converse, they tend to use contractions and do not always speak in complete sentences. Your scripts should mirror this conversational style. Let me suggest some differences:

Written Language	*Spoken Language*
I am going	I'm going *or* I'm gonna
They will probably	They'll probably
It is obvious	It's obvious
No thank you	No thanks *or* Nah

Use Action Verbs. I mentioned this earlier, but let me expand on it here. Generally speaking, it is more interesting to use the active case with verbs, not the passive case.

Passive Case	*Active Case*
Mary *was loved* by John.	John loved Mary.
The South was defeated by the North.	The North *defeated* the South.
Ice cream *is liked* by most kids.	Most kids *like* ice cream.

The passive case involves some form of the verb *to be* along with another verb. This is much weaker and blander than writing using active verbs.

Use Repetition Carefully. In certain cases, when you wish to establish a dramatic effect, repetition is fine, but you must be careful not to overdo it (or to use it without recognizing you are doing so) because it can quickly become boring.

Use Teasers and Hooks in Moderation. Teasers and hooks are devices—like questions or minidramas or statements or quotations—that have some kind of shock value. We use them to attract listeners, to catch their attention, but we have to be careful we don't overdo things when we use them, and that we use them in an appropriate manner. We must avoid appearing (or being, I would add) sensationalistic and doing anything to get attention.

Have a Strong Closing. This is crucial. The script has to have a good ending, one that seems logical and is satisfying to listeners and viewers. That is, you can't just end a script suddenly, because you've run out of time (for example, in some assignment in which you have to produce a script that will last a certain amount of time). Let me offer an analogy. Many of us are used to ending our dinners with desserts; we feel somewhat uncomfortable, somehow, if we don't have a dessert to conclude our dinner. In the same light, a script has to lead to some kind of a logical, reasonable, satisfactory ending or resolution. Otherwise, the audience is left hanging in the air, so to speak.

Follow the Specifications for the Script. If the script is for a 30-second commercial, make sure your script takes only 30 seconds—not 43 seconds (because you couldn't get everything in that you wanted to). If the script is for a public service announcement, make sure you are not (without recognizing it, perhaps) writing a commercial. In radio and television, time is crucial (and time is money, as well), and you've got to be precise when it comes to the length of a script. So the rule here is read the specifications for the script (or the assignment) very carefully and make certain that you understand what you are supposed to do.

One problem students sometimes face is that they *think* they understand what an assignment is, but when they sit down to write they find, suddenly, that they are confused. One of the biggest problems teachers face is that they *think* they have explained an assignment clearly and students *think* they understand an assignment, but, at times, both students and teachers are mistaken. All we can do, in the face of this dilemma, is work harder and try to communicate with one another more clearly and more effectively. Language is very slippery. It is the ambiguity in language that makes it so powerful, but it is also something that can lead people astray.

Radio Script Formats

Now that we have an understanding of how we write for the ear, let us take a look at the matter of script formats. I will start with the basic format for radio scripts. Here are some general principles to follow when writing a radio script. Not everyone follows these rules, I might add, but they are commonly used.

(1) Divide the page into two columns: instructions on the left and dialogue on the right.

(2) Names of characters and directions for music, sound effects, and so on are all given in the left-hand column, double-spaced, and written in ALL CAPS. *Everything except dialogue is written in all caps and single-spaced.* This column takes approximately a third of the page.

(3) Dialogue is written only in the right-hand column. *Dialogue is always double-spaced and written in Caps and Lowercase* (like typical prose). Dialogue is shown in caps and lowercase to differentiate it from instructions. This means that actors and actresses and production people can tell, at a glance, what is dialogue and what isn't.

(4) Instructions about how a line is to be read are in parentheses as well as ALL CAPS and shown in the right-hand side of the script in appropriate places.

(5) Directions for music and sound effects are not only shown in ALL CAPS, but are also UNDERLINED.

We can see now why the convention of having everything but dialogue in all caps is so important. In the right-hand side of the script we find dialogue, instructions to actors and actresses, sound effects, and music—all of which must be easily and instantaneously differentiated from the dialogue and from one another. We do this visually (that is, typographically), using the differences between ALL CAPS and Caps and Lowercase and ALL CAPS and ALL CAPS UNDERLINED to help us.

Exhibit 2.1 is a sample radio script that shows how the rules described above are implemented. The terms used in the script are explained in Exhibit 2.2.

This sample shows what a typical radio script looks like and uses the conventions described earlier. (The script, incidentally, is for a kind of feature known as an "anniversary" story, which would be produced on the anniversary of some important or interesting event.) As you can see, radio scripts are relatively simple in design or structure, but they can have a very powerful impact due to the ability of performers to stimulate our imaginations and the ability of music and sound effects to provide a semblance of reality.

Exhibit 2.1: Sample Radio Script

MUSIC	<u>BACH PRELUDE UP AND OUT</u>
SFX	<u>COMPUTERS BEING KEYBOARDED . . .</u> <u>CLICK, CLICK . . .</u>
NARRATOR	It's Friday, the 13th, 1990, . . . the fifth anniversary of that dreaded day when computer viruses started destroying files all over the country.
SFX	<u>COMPUTER SOUNDS . . .</u> <u>WILD BEEPING</u>
NARRATOR	Take the case of Professor James Smith, for example.
SMITH	(EXCITEDLY) What's happening to my computer? What happened to my files? Something crazy is going on here.
NARRATOR	Computer viruses are programs that malevolent people insert into other programs . . . these viruses do anything from playing songs to eating up files.
SFX	<u>COMPUTER VOICE SINGING: GOD</u> <u>BLESS AMERICA. FADES UNDER.</u>
SMITH	(RESIGNED VOICE) The virus ate up a number of my files. Fortunately, I'd copied them . . . but it took me hours to kill that blasted virus.
NARRATOR	These viruses were created by people known as hackers. They love to play around with computers and sometimes, in their zeal to show their power and mastery, they get into trouble. Let's meet one whose nom de plume is John Q. Public.

(continued)

Exhibit 2.1 Continued

JOHN Q. PUBLIC	(VOICE OF ADOLESCENT) I've been hacking for six years, now. I've got into the U.S. Army panglobal computer network, Science-net and all kinds of other networks. It's fun. And I created a virus that plays "God Bless America." But it doesn't destroy any files.
SFX	POLICE SIRENS BLARING AWAY. FADE.
NARRATOR	The police thought otherwise, when they swooped down on the house where this young man lived one evening to arrest him.
MUSIC	COMPUTER MUSIC . . . GOD BLESS AMERICA. UP AND UNDER.
SFX	KNOCKING ON DOOR.
POLICE	(ASSERTIVELY) Open up, this is the police . . .

Exhibit 2.2: Commonly Used Terms in Radio Production

on mike	Performer speaks at microphone.
off mike	Performer speaks away from microphone.
fading on	Performer moves toward microphone.
fading off	Performer moves away from microphone.
behind obstruction	Performer speaks from behind something.
filter mike	Performer sounds as if on telephone.
echo chamber	Performer seems to be in huge room.
segue	Smooth transition from one sound to another.
blend	More than one sound heard at same time.
cut or switch	Rapid alternation from one sound to another.
fade in/ fade out	Making sound volume greater or smaller.
up and out	Volume rises and then fades out.

Radio as Theater of the Mind

Radio, as I pointed out earlier, is sometimes described as the theater of the mind or the theater of the imagination. (Television has been called the theater of the mindless.) This is because radio unleashes our power of imagination so easily. All that is needed is a good script, some decent narration, some good acting, some realistic sound effects, some special effects, and a bit of music. With these few elements, all kinds of incredible things are possible.

As an example of radio's power, let me cite the famous broadcast of H. G. Wells's science fiction masterwork, *War of the Worlds*, which was broadcast on CBS's Mercury Theatre of the Air on October 30, 1938, and described a Martian invasion of America. This broadcast led to a panic. Here is how Sharon Lowery and Melvin L. DeFleur describe the phenomenon in their book *Milestones in Mass Communication Research: Media Effects* (1983):

> Because the dramatization was presented in a clever newscast style, many listeners believed that the Martians were actually taking over. Others were driven to mindless panic because the invasion seemed a direct threat to their lives. Many thought the world was ending; terrified people cried, hid, prayed, or fled into the countryside. The panic was, of course, an accident; there was no intent to frighten anyone. Nevertheless, what occurred that October night was one of the most remarkable media events of all time. If nothing else was proved that night, it was demonstrated to many that radio could have a powerful impact on its audience. (p. 59)

This broadcast was the subject of a celebrated study, called *The Invasion from Mars*, by a distinguished sociologist, Hadley Cantril. His book includes the script of the story, as well. Even though an announcer indicated that the program was a dramatization, for a variety of reasons large numbers of people forgot that they were listening to a play and believed that Martians had actually invaded America.

After a small portion of a Tchaikovsky piano concerto was played, and faded out, introductions were made. An announcer stated that a dramatization of Wells's *War of the Worlds* would be heard. And about a minute into the program, Orson Welles's brilliant narration began. (It was based on H. G. Wells's prose, though Welles made a few changes.) Notice how beautifully it was written:

> We know now that in the early years of the twentieth century, this world was being watched by intelligences greater than man's and yet as mortal as his own. We know now that as human beings busied themselves about their various concerns they were scrutinized and studied, perhaps almost as narrowly as a man with a microscope might scrutinize the transient creatures that swarm and multiply in a drop of water. With infinite complacence people went to and fro over the earth about their little affairs, serene in their assurance of their dominion over this small spinning fragment of solar driftwood which by chance or design man has inherited out of the dark mystery of Time and Space. Yet across an immense ethereal gulf minds that are to our minds as ours are to the beasts in the jungle, intellects vast, cool, and unsympathetic regarded this earth with envious eyes and slowly and surely drew their plans against us.

This opening narration brilliantly sets the scene and establishes a mood and sense of menace and threat that, it turned out, large numbers of people found convincing. Drama usually involves what has been called a "willing suspension of disbelief" in people; in the case of this broadcast, people actually panicked.

There is another famous example of the power of radio, one that is much less anxiety provoking. I am referring to Stan Freberg's famous disquisition on the power of radio, in which he has a gigantic maraschino cherry dropped into a lake full of whipped cream. His point is that people can imagine something like this very easily, and can see it in their "mind's eye"; were this scene to be produced for film or television, on the other hand, it would cost a great deal of money and would probably not be very effective. (The following radio spot, copyright 1964 by the Radio Advertising Bureau, is used with permission.)

FREBERG:	Okay people, now when I give the cue, I want the 700-foot mountain of whipped cream to roll into Lake Michigan, which has been drained and filled with hot chocolate. Then the Royal Canadian Air Force will fly overhead, towing a ten-ton maraschino cherry which will be dropped into the whipped cream to the cheering of 25,000 extras.
FREBERG:	All right, cue the mountain.
SFX:	(CREAKS, GROANS, PROLONGED SPLASH)
FREBERG:	Cue the Air Force.
SFX:	(PROPELLERS ROAR INTO AND PAST MIKE; WING STRUTS WHINE)
FREBERG:	Cue the maraschino cherry.
SFX:	(SCREAMING, WHISTLING FALL, AND LARGE PLOP)
FREBERG:	Okay, 25,000 cheering extras.
SFX:	(PROLONGED AND TUMULTUOUS OVATION)
FREBERG:	Now—you want to try that on television?
SPONSOR:	Wel-l-l-l,
FREBERG:	You see, radio's a very special medium because it stretches the imagination.
SPONSOR:	Doesn't television stretch the imagination?
FREBERG:	Up to 21 inches—yes.

A Note on the Radio Industry

The 1930s and early 1940s were radio's greatest years; after that, as television took center stage, radio changed, and although it remains, in certain respects, a powerful influence and is a very profitable medium, it has become, I would argue, an audio wasteland for the most part. Once radio was full of wonderful comedy shows and great adventure programs. Now it functions essentially as a background medium, with many different kinds of music stations, some all-news stations, and very little else. Except for National Public Radio, some alternative stations, and some college stations here and there, radio has become a disaster area. Thus radio, which once was our dominant medium, has now become little more than an individualized jukebox for most Americans. There are, of course, some excellent programs to be found on occasion, but radio is not living up to its potential.

Television Documentary Script Formats

There are no universally followed rules for formatting television scripts (or any kind of script, for that matter). What follows are suggestions for designing documentary script formats that I believe are reasonable and logical.

(1) Divide the page in half. Video is given in the left-hand side, audio (and dialogue) the right-hand side. It is customary to write the words *video* and *audio* at the top of each page.

(2) ALL MATERIAL ON THE VIDEO SIDE IS TYPED IN CAPITALS. This involves such matters as instructions, kinds of camera shots, and the like.

(3) Dialogue is always double-spaced in Cap and Lowercase letters on the right-hand side of the page, the audio side. Everything else is ALL CAPS.

(4) CHARACTER NAMES ARE TYPED ALL CAPS AND SHOWN ON THE AUDIO SIDE.

(5) SOUND EFFECTS AND MUSIC ARE EACH GIVEN SEPARATE LINES and are shown on the audio side.

(6) PHYSICAL MOVEMENTS ARE SHOWN IN ALL CAPS ON THE VIDEO SIDE.

See Exhibit 2.3 for an excerpt from a documentary script that follows these formatting rules.

Television programs usually begin with the instructions "fade up" and end with instructions to "fade out." The documentary starts with a long shot of three strippers and the sound of disco rock. The long shot enables viewers to get a sense of context. Then we move in to a medium shot and cut quickly to two close-up shots of individual strippers. Then we dissolve to a medium close-up, which is followed by having the camera

Exhibit 2.3: Example of a Documentary Script Format

What follows is a sampling of a documentary script—showing how video and dialogue are integrated. I will discuss important aspects of the script, which was written by one of my students, Anna Geddes.

VIDEO	AUDIO
FADE UP ON MS OF THREE MALE STRIPPERS ONSTAGE AT DIMLY LIT, PLUSH, NIGHTCLUB. THERE ARE MIR-RORS ON WALLS AND FLASHY OUTFITS.	(FADE UP ON FAST-PACED DISCO ROCK MUSIC ACCOM-PANIED BY SOUNDS OF WOMEN SCREAMING AND LAUGHING.)
MS OF STRIPPERS ON TABLE WITH WOMEN CROWDING AROUND HIM.	
CUT TO CU OF STRIPPER #2.	
CUT TO CU OF STRIPPER #3.	
DISSOLVE TO MCU AND PAN OF TABLE AS STRIPPER COMES OVER AND COLLECTS TIPS.	
DISSOLVE BACK TO MS OF THREE STRIPPERS. THIS SHOT IS IN SLOW MOTION WHICH SLIGHTLY BLURS THE IMAGE AND ADDS A BLUE HAZE TO IT. CAMERA ARCS IN A SEMI-CIRCLE TO SHOW ENTIRE ACTION.	(CROSSFADE MUSIC WITH SOUND EFFECTS: A DEEP, OMINOUS BASS GUITAR CHORD. SFX OUT.) (LORETTA) Women can fi-nally do some of the naughty things men have been doing for years. (LYNN) I didn't think it would be a turn-on, but boy, is my husband in for a surprise to-night.

(continued)

Exhibit 2.3 Continued

VIDEO	AUDIO
KEY TITLE: MALE REVELA-TIONS.	(SFX: DEEP, OMINOUS BASS GUITAR CHORD. SFX OUT AS NARRATOR SAYS "LADIES' NIGHT FEATUR-ING. . . ." MUSIC FADES UP AND OUT.)
LOSE KEY.	
DISSOLVE TO LS OF A STREET WITH MANY BRIGHTLY COLORED SIGNS FOR MALE STRIP SHOWS. THE SHOT IS MOVING (ON TOP OF A VEHICLE) AND PANS SEVERAL NIGHTCLUBS.	(NARRATOR) In the past few years a novel erotic style of enter-tainment has gained a wide and wild audience.

---

pan a scene in which a stripper collects tips at a table. All of this is to catch the attention of the viewer.

In this section of the script, we are told the title of the documentary—*Male Revelations.* This is a catchy and clever title, which plays upon several meanings of the word *revelations.* We usually use it to mean revealing things about oneself, but here it also means physically revealing oneself. Then we are introduced to some women who discuss their feelings about these clubs and the narrator, who establishes a context for the documentary. The author does an excellent job of attracting our attention and getting us involved and interested in the documentary.

Documentary Writing Techniques

Here are some of the most common components of documentaries.

Narration. The narrator sets the stage and helps provide continuity, leading viewers from one scene or interview to the next. The amount of narration should be limited. In a documentary, characters should tell their stories and provide most of the information. The narrator should weave things together, not dominate the documentary.

Voice-Overs. Here the narrator or a character speaks but is not shown on camera. Instead, he or she provides commentary or explains something that we see on the screen. Voice-overs should be limited and essentially used to move things along.

Interviews. Here, characters speak for themselves. It is not necessary to have all interviews tied to questions asked by some narrator. While interviewees talk about things, generally in response to some question asked by a narrator, what the interviewees say often stands alone. A constant pattern of question and answer can make a documentary boring. There should be a number of people interviewed and shown on camera in a documentary, all with different perspectives on things. If only one person is interviewed, we don't have a documentary (as I see it), but an interview. Others have different opinions about this matter, I might add. In many cases what we might describe as *on-scene events* are important. If one is doing a documentary about professional wrestling, for example, it makes sense to shoot some scenes at wrestling matches to give viewers a sense of what these events are like.

Graphics. People should be identified with their names keyed in and then faded out. Viewers like to know who they are watching. When appropriate, places should also be identified. It is also useful, in certain situations, to use charts and diagrams, which show relationships very quickly and convey information efficiently. In certain cases, maps and photographs are also helpful.

Music. Music is also useful, in places, to help establish a mood.

Natural Sound and Sound Effects. In many cases, natural sound (the sound one hears when interviewing people or visiting places) is enough, but in some cases, sound effects can be used to augment natural sound.

The terms in Exhibit 2.4 represent the "grammar" of television and are the means by which documentaries (and television programs in general) are structured. It is a good exercise to watch television programs in terms of the way they are edited—to see how the director uses cuts, dissolves, superimpositions, and other techniques to create particular effects. These editing techniques are used in conjunction with various kinds of camera shots, which are described in Exhibit 2.5.

It is important to vary the camera shots used (otherwise the viewer becomes bored) and to use them with some degree of logic. Television viewers learn certain video conventions (as the result of years of exposure) and become irritated if these conventions are not adhered to—if the visual aspects of a program are, somehow, strange.

What is reproduced in Exhibit 2.3 is the first page of a 12-page documentary. In the remaining pages of this script, the author has the two women, Loretta and Lynn, discuss their feelings about the experience of watching male strippers, has interviews with a professor (a sociologist who has written on male strippers), with a number of male strippers (and shows the sociologist interviewing some male strippers), and with a radio personality and author who has written a book on male strippers.

The author of this script, we see, brings to bear a number of different perspectives on the male stripping phenomenon—perspectives gathered by research. This documentary, like all good documentaries, is based on research. (What a documentary is and how documentaries can be used in teaching will be discussed later, in the section on television documentaries.)

This script has a number of characteristics found in good documentaries:

(1) *It has visual complexity.* A number of different kinds of shots are used and the variety of shots used is good. It is boring, visually speaking, to have the same kind of shot shown all the time. This script uses visual images as well as sound and music very effectively.

Exhibit 2.4: Basic Editing Techniques Used in TV Production

fade in	Picture slowly forms from black (blank) screen.
fade out	Picture slowly disappears to black (blank) screen.
dissolve	As one picture fades, another is created.
cut	Immediate transition from one picture to another.
superimposition	One picture imposed on another for brief period.
wipe	Picture is eliminated from a particular direction (vertical, horizontal, diagonal).
split screen	Separate images on each half of screen.
film and slides	Film clips or slides. Must be keyed in script.
key	One image inserted over another: words over picture

(2) *It has intellectual complexity.* The author bases the script on a variety of different perspectives on the phenomenon of male stripping—there are interviews with fans, with scholars, with writers, and with strippers.

(3) *It weaves the interviews in, back and forth, with one another.* In simplistic scripts, people are interviewed and, so to speak, dropped or dispatched. In this script, interviewees keep appearing and reappearing, creating a kind of "dialogue" with one another on the phenomenon of male stripping.

(4) *It is not overnarrated.* The narrator in this script holds things together and allows the interviewees to carry the burden of the story. The narrator does not tell the story, just using interviewees for sound bites, visual interest, or reinforcement (of the narrator's position). The narrator, then, coordinates things and allows the people being interviewed to speak for themselves.

Exercises

1. Write a three- or four-page radio script that gives an idea of one or more of the following: your interests, your background,

Exhibit 2.5: Kinds of Camera Shots

extreme close-up (ECU)	Face fills screen.
close-up (CU)	Shot of face and neck.
medium close-up (MCU)	Shot of face and upper part of the body.
medium shot (MS)	Shot of an individual or small group.
full shot (FS)	Full view of performer.
long shot (LS)	Setting shown to orient viewer.
extreme long shot (ELS)	Setting and general area shown.
2 shot, 3 shot	Two people, three people shown.
over the shoulder (OTS)	Shot from behind, above performer's shoulder.
surveying pan (SP)	Camera passes (pans) across scene.
cut in (CI)	Camera moves in for close-up detail.
cut away (CA)	Camera moves away to different scene.
zoom in (ZI)	Camera lens moves in on something.
zoom out (ZO)	Camera lens moves back from something.
reaction shot (RS)	Camera shows reaction of someone to something.

your goals, your talents, and what you are like. This script should have "full production values," which means it should have a narrator (if needed), actors and actresses, and appropriate sound effects and music. Perform the script, using classmates to play various parts. The script should have three to five performers in it (this is to prevent you from writing monologues). Use your imagination and inventiveness. No holds barred—but no profanity and nothing that would offend any group of people, of course.

2. Record a television documentary on a VCR and, on a piece of paper, note the various technical matters that have been discussed above about television scripts—the kinds of camera shots, the editing techniques used (cuts, dissolves), the use of sound, the use of keyed titles, and so on. Compare this with a televised portion of a football game or a baseball game. What do you learn from looking at television from a technical point of view?

3. Try writing a television script. Write a one-page script for one (or all) of the following topics: journal writing, mornings in my life, a hobby, "let me teach you something."

M. JOURDAIN: . . . I must commit a secret to you. I'm in love with a person of great quality, and I should be glad if you would help me write something to her in a short *billet-doux,* which I'll drop at her feet.

PHILOSOPHY-MASTER: Very well . . . Is it verse that you would write to her?

M. JOURDAIN: No, no, none of your verse.

PHILOSOPHY-MASTER: You would only have prose?

M. JOURDAIN: No, I would neither have verse nor prose.

PHILOSOPHY-MASTER: It must be one or t'other.

M. JOURDAIN: Why so?

PHILOSOPHY-MASTER: Because, sir, there's nothing to express one's self by, but prose, or verse.

M. JOURDAIN: Is there nothing then but prose, or verse?

PHILOSOPHY-MASTER: No, sir, whatever is not prose, is verse, and whatever is not verse, is prose.

M. JOURDAIN: And when one talks, what may that be then?

PHILOSOPHY-MASTER: Prose.

—Moliere, *The Bourgeois Gentleman*, Act II, Scene 6

3

Comedy Writing

Humor is one of the most important elements in writing, and good comedy writers are worth their weight in gold. It is frequently said that you can't teach people to be funny, or to write good comedy. This is not true—most of the time.

There are, as I see things, four possibilities here—as far as writing comedy is concerned. First, there are people who can't write well and don't have a good sense of humor. They can't write good comedy. Second, there are people who can't write well but have a good sense of humor, so if they could write well, they would be good comedy writers. Third, there are people who can write well, but don't have much of a sense of humor. And fourth, there are people who write well and have an excellent sense of humor. They make the best comedy writers.

Throw Away Your Joke Books

The first thing you have to do is throw away your joke books. Jokes are a form of humor—more precisely, jokes can be defined as "narratives or stories with punch lines that are meant to amuse." When you tell a joke you are performing someone else's material. If you aren't a good performer or if your joke is stale (and most become so very quickly), it doesn't make sense for you to tell jokes. But even if you do tell jokes very well, or can write them into a script, there's something static and artificial about telling jokes.

Why limit yourself to one narrow form of humor when there are so many techniques of humor you can use to create original material?

The Why of Humor

We don't know why people laugh. This is an enigma that has occupied our greatest thinkers, from Aristotle to Kant, from Hobbes to Freud—and to this day nobody has been able to figure out why we laugh. There are, broadly speaking, a few commonly held theories about why we laugh. First, there are the *superiority* theorists, such as Aristotle and Hobbes, who argue that we laugh because we feel superior to others (those at whom we laugh). Aristotle said comedy is based on "an imitation of men worse than the average," and defined comedy as "a dramatic picture of the Ridiculous."

Second, there are the *incongruity* theorists, such as the French philosopher Henri Bergson. He suggested that humor involves "something mechanical encrusted on the living." These theorists argue that humor involves some kind of surprising difference between what you expect and what you get. This theory, in one form or another, is probably the most commonly advanced explanation of why we laugh.

Third, there are *psychoanalytic* theories, such as those of Freud, which argue that humor involves masked aggression (often of a sexual as well as hostile nature) and suggest that we enjoy humor because we can take pleasure in the aggression without feeling guilty about doing so. Humor, from this perspective, is tied to unconscious processes. Freud wrote a book on this subject, *Jokes and Their Relation to the Unconscious*, which explains his ideas.

Finally, there are what might be called *cognitive* theorists, such as Gregory Bateson, who argue that humor involves such things as paradox and may be too complex for the human mind to figure out at this stage of our development. There are probably fifty or a hundred theories of humor—by psychologists, anthropologists, philosophers, sociologists, psychiatrists, and others.

To be a comedy writer, you do not need a theory that explains why people laugh. What you need to know is what makes people laugh. There's a difference.

The 45 Techniques of Humor

In order to find out what makes people laugh, I made a content analysis of every example of humor I could get my hands on: plays, novels, comic books, joke books, cartoons, films. I wasn't concerned with why something was funny, but, instead, with what the author did that generated humor.

From this content analysis I came up with the 45 techniques listed below. These are, I believe, the fundamental methods used by all humorists to make people laugh. Frequently a number of them will be used together.

Language	Logic	Identity	Visual
allusion	absurdity	before/after	chase
bombast	accident	burlesque	speed
definition	analogy	caricature	slapstick
exaggeration	catalogue	eccentricity	
facetiousness	coincidence	embarrassment	
insults	comparison	exposure	
infantilism	disappointment	grotesque	
irony	ignorance	imitation	
misunderstanding	mistakes	impersonation	
overliteralness	repetition	mimicry	
puns and	reversal	parody	
wordplay	rigidity	scale	
repartee	theme/variation	stereotypes	
ridicule		unmasking	
sarcasm			
satire			

When I had isolated the 45 techniques, I noticed that they fell under the four categories into which they are divided here: humor of language, humor of identity, humor of logic, and a fourth category that involves visual matters (in which the humor is physical). I believe that any example of humor, whether taken from an ancient Greek comedy, Shakespeare, a French film, a Johnny Carson monologue, a situation comedy, or a stand-up comedian, can be shown to use one or more of these techniques.

And I have not been able to find any other techniques to add to my list, though I'm still looking. When people write comedy they do not, consciously, think about the techniques they are using. I doubt that any comedy writers are even aware of most of these techniques. What happens is that they "feel" (based on past experience) that in a given situation, something is called for.

Comedy writers figure out, on their own, a number of these various techniques, but they don't articulate them or bring them to consciousness. It's like driving: When you learn to drive you have to do a number of things you're not used to doing, and at the same time, but after you've driven for a while, all the steps become second nature to you.

You can take this list of techniques and analyze Shakespeare's *Twelfth Night,* for example. What you will find is that Shakespeare was a master who used many different techniques: There are grotesque (funny) characters, there is wordplay, there is unmasking, there is revelation, there is facetiousness—one could go on and on.

Some of these techniques are used more often than others. Let me list and briefly explain what might be described as the most fundamental techniques used in comedy writing. Some of the techniques, let me add, are easy to understand, but some demand a bit of explanation.

Basic Comedy Writing Techniques

Parody. A parody is a comic imitation of another person's style of writing (such as that of Ernest Hemingway) or of a genre (or kind) of writing (such as the James Bond spy story or the Western or the college bulletin). When you write a parody, you must be certain that you make fun of something that is distinctive and easily identified. You must also use a number of other techniques of humor: exaggeration, facetiousness, wordplay, and as many others as you can manage.

Here is a selection from a Woody Allen parody of college bulletins taken from "Spring Bulletin," which appeared in the *New Yorker* (April 29, 1967):

Philosophy I: Everyone from Plato to Camus is read and the following topics are covered: Ethics: The categorical imperative and six
ways to make it work for you. Aesthetics: Is art the mirror of life,
or what? Metaphysics: What happens to the soul after death? How
does it manage? Epistemology: Is knowledge knowable? If not,
how do we know this? The Absurd: Why existence is often considered silly, particularly for men who wear brown and white shoes.
Manyness and oneness are studied as they relate to otherness.
(Students achieving oneness will move ahead to twoness.)

This parody does not seem too far removed from the example
found earlier in this book of college bulletin prose taken from
the Harvard catalog.

Exhibit 3.1 provides another example of parody, this time of
soap operas, in a brief selection from Bob Elliot and Ray
Goulding's *From Approximately Coast to Coast . . . It's the Bob &
Ray Show* (1985, pp. 62-63).

Exaggeration. This is a standard technique in comedy writing—
found, for example, in rather pure form in tall tales, but pervad-
ing all humor. It can also take other forms, such as having
characters who are very tall or very short (we are close to the
grotesque here) or characters who are nonstop talkers or won't
say anything. That is, the exaggeration need not always be
verbal—though that is its most common form. Exaggeration is
often tied to insult.

Punning and Wordplay. Here we find writers using the "sound"
of words to create humor. Puns are supposed to be "the lowest
form of wit," but a good pun is really an excellent form of
humor. It is lousy puns that give this technique a bad name.

Here is an example of some first-class punning—in which the
puns are not forced and are relevant to the topics being discussed.

A wit couldn't help himself but made puns on all occasions. On
being taken to an orphan asylum, he said "This far and no father."
The next morning, at breakfast, he declared, biting into a roll, "The
bun is the lowest form of wheat." Finally, his friends thought they
could silence him by taking him to see the Grand Canyon. He
gazed at it for a while and said, "Gorgeous, isn't it."

Exhibit 3.1: Bob and Ray Script

DRAMATIC
THEME MUSIC:
ESTABLISH
AND UNDER FOR

BOB: Welcome again to Garish Summit and its endless story of intrigue among the socially prominent. There—in stately splendor far removed from the squalid village below—the beautiful people fight their petty battles over power and money.

BOB: As our action begins, strong-willed Agatha Murchfield is in the solarium awaiting the arrival of her lawyer, Bodin Pardew. . . .

AGATHA: . . . I have something preying on my mind that I need your help with, Bodin. A man has turned up here in Garish Summit who claims to be my long-lost elder son, Caldwell.

PARDEW: That's shocking, Agatha. We've known each other for forty years and I always thought your weak-willed son, Rodney, was an only child.

AGATHA: Well, I thought so, too. That's the strange part I don't understand.

PARDEW: Well, you're a fabulously rich widow who's inherited the world's largest chain of lead mines. The man's probably a fortune hunter.

Impersonation and Dialects. It's hard to say why we find dialects and accents amusing, but we do. It may be that dialects make us feel superior (because we speak, we all believe, the way God intended for people to speak). It probably is because there are elements of impersonation and mimicry involved in dialect. Whatever the case, dialect is a useful means of generating humor—provided that the dialect is tied to the people being imitated. That is, the dialect must be used to satirize the people or deal with commonly held comic stereotypes about them.

There's nothing terribly funny about having a character speak with a Russian accent. But if we throw in allusions to the KGB, the Communist party, being sent to Siberia, the Red Army, long lines people wait in to get food and goods, and other matters connected with Russian politics, society, character, and culture, then dialect can be very effective.

Insults. We must be very careful with insults—a form of humor in which the aggression is extremely obvious. One should never insult any ethnic, religious, sexual, or racial group or do anything that would offend them. This leaves us with only certain targets that are acceptable: occupational groups (professors, lawyers, psychiatrists), political groups (Democrats, Republicans), citizens of particular countries (the French, the English), public figures, mothers-in-law, and so on. One must be very careful; the basic rule is: When in doubt, leave it out.

Johnny Carson's monologues are full of insults—some direct and others veiled, by allusions to stupid things people have done. Here is an example from Shakespeare's *Henry IV, Part I:* Act II, Scene 4, in which Henry and Falstaff are insulting each other. Henry is talking about how fat Falstaff is and Falstaff is describing how thin Henry is:

> *Prince:* I'll be no longer guilty of this sin. This sanguine coward, this bed-presser, this horseback breaker, the huge hill of flesh—
> *Falstaff:* S'blood, you starveling, you eel-skin, you dried neat's tongue, you bull's pizzle [penis], you stockfish! O for breath to utter what is like thee! You tailor's yard, you sheath, you bowcase, you vile standing tuck.

Notice that one method Falstaff uses is comparison; he suggests that Henry is as thin as a tailor's yardstick or a sheath. Invidious comparisons are an excellent way of making insults.

Ridicule. This is a form of linguistic humor that derides, makes fun of, or attempts to humiliate some person, practice, or idea. In the passage that follows, from *Miss Lonelyhearts* (1959),

Nathanael West has one of his characters, Shrike, ridicule the life-style of the hedonist.

> You dedicate your life to the pursuit of pleasure. No overindulgence, mind you, but knowing that your body is a pleasure machine you treat it carefully in order to get the most out of it. Gold as well as booze, Philadelphia Jack O'Brien and his chestweights as well as Spanish dancers. Nor do you neglect the pleasures of the mind. You fornicate under pictures by Matisse and Picasso, you drink from Renaissance glassware, and often you spend an evening beside the fireplace with Proust and an apple. At last, after much good fun, the day comes when you realize that soon you must die. You invite all your old mistresses, trainers, artists and boon companions. The guests are dressed in black . . . the table is a coffin carved for you by Eric Gill. You serve caviar and blackberries and licorice candy and coffee without cream. After the dancing girls have finished, you get to your feet and call for silence in order to explain your philosophy of life. (pp. 60-61)

This passage, one of the greatest displays of stylistic brilliance in American comic literature, deserves study. How does West achieve his effects? What, in particular, generates the humor?

Mistakes. Mistakes are a common method of generating humor. (They are different from misunderstandings, which involve language.) People make mistakes for a variety of reasons: bad judgment, inattention, lack of knowledge, stupidity. Whatever the reason, mistakes—and their consequences—are one of the main means of creating humor. Shakespeare's *Comedy of Errors* is a good example of how mistakes can be used for comic purposes.

Eccentricity and Deviation. Here we have characters who have one or more of the following attributes: zany, grotesque, oddball, monomaniacal, weird. People who violate the norms of behavior in a given culture, in harmless ways, are the source of much humor. They may have a single, all-consuming passion (gluttony, butterflies, whatever), they may have delusions of grandeur, they may be wacky. Whatever the case, they provide useful foils and can be exploited for comic purposes.

What follows is a passage from one of the masterpieces of "the theater of the absurd," Ionesco's *The Bald Soprano* (1958, p. 11).

```
MR. SMITH:    All doctors are quacks. And all pa-
              tients, too. Only the Royal Navy is
              honest in England.
MRS. SMITH:   But not sailors.
MR. SMITH:    Naturally. (A pause. Still reading
              his paper.) Here's a thing I don't
              understand. In the newspaper they al-
              ways give the age of deceased per-
              sons but never the age of the newly
              born. That doesn't make sense.
```

Ionesco's play makes fun of logic and rationality and has characters who behave in an "absurd" way. A great deal of humor has an absurd quality about it, but I use the term in reference to logical absurdity and the characters and the situations found in the theater of the absurd.

On Humorous Techniques

There are a couple of things that should be mentioned here, relative to the 45 humorous techniques listed earlier. First, in many cases, the techniques can be reversed to good effect. Thus exaggeration can be reversed to yield understatement and insults can be directed toward oneself, yielding "victim" humor. Second, the techniques often are all mixed together. For example, in the insults that Henry and Falstaff hurl at each other, Falstaff also uses invidious comparisons.

Invidious comparisons can also be used for "victim" humor. I wrote an analysis of some of the classic television shows of the 1970s in a book called *The TV-Guided American*. A review of this book, by Jeff Greenfield, appeared in the *New York Times Book Review* and concluded with the following statement: "Berger is to the analysis of television what Idi Amin is to tourism in Uganda!" I use this "insult" to great effect in lectures I give. It always draws a big laugh and creates a certain amount of sympathy in my audiences.

One cannot automatically decide to use certain of the techniques and go about making humor in an "automatic" manner (though a joke writer I know does so, cranking out 50 jokes a day to sell to disk jockeys). What happens is that certain of the techniques are most suitable for certain types of people who feel comfortable with these techniques and develop their proficiency in using them.

You cannot write humor (or anything else) mechanically, but if you are aware of the techniques that are the building blocks of all humor, you can learn to use and adapt some of them and create, if you have enough imagination and inventiveness, and a command of the English language, some really excellent comedy. Some of my students have done so, and if they can, anyone can (comedy of insult)!

Exercises

1. Write a radio script of 300 to 350 words of dialogue that parodies some of the following:

Star Trek	Westerns	soap operas
James Bond	*Star Wars*	game shows

2. Pretend you are a television reviewer. Write a mock review of a mixed-genre show—that is, a show that combines any two or three of the following genres (for example, you might design a combination news and soap opera program, a science fiction game show, or a sports/nature program).

news	talk show	sports	soap opera
commercial	game show	science fiction	action-adventure
sitcom	drama	nature	interview

Insert made-up segments from the show in your review.

3. Analyze Shakespeare's *Twelfth Night* using the 45 techniques. Make a chart listing the techniques and the places in the play where each technique is used. In addition, analyze *Saturday Night Live*, a Johnny Carson monologue, and a situation comedy.

4. Do the Comedy Calculator Experiment, as described below. I have argued that techniques are basic to creating humor and writing good comedy, not telling jokes. Let me demonstrate this by showing that jokes generate humor by using the various techniques listed in Exhibit 3.2.

To make things a bit easier, I've listed the various techniques alphabetically and added a list of typical subjects of jokes: psychiatrists, professors, the clergy, and so on.

The Comedy Calculator Experiment. What I will do, in this parody of scientific analysis, is deconstruct a joke. I will show the basic techniques operating in the joke—techniques that, I've argued, exist in all forms and all examples of humor. I will reduce the joke to a formula, based on the subject matter and the techniques of humor that create the humor in the joke.

I've chosen a joke because jokes are short and easy to use—but you could use the chart and techniques to analyze any example of humor you want to, from comic strips to Shakespeare. In using the Comedy Calculator, do the following:

(a) Determine the subject of the joke (example, marriage, or MAR).
(b) List the techniques, by number, in order of importance (example, 25/17/2). Here is a joke, which I will analyze:

> A priest was walking down the street when two hippies who knew him came over to say hello. The priest was heavily bandaged, so one hippie asked him how he got hurt. "I slipped in my bath," said the priest. The hippies said they were sorry he had hurt himself and hoped he would recover quickly and then walked away. A block down the street the first hippie turned to the second and asked, "What's a bath?" "How should I know?" said the second hippie. "I ain't Catholic."

The most important element in this joke is religion, which is what the punch line is based on, so I would say the subject is religion. The basic comedic technique in the joke, I would suggest, is stereotyping: There is a typical stereotype of hippies as somewhat "dirty." The joke also ridicules them for their ignorance, technique 21 ("What's a bath?"), and mistakenly assuming baths are connected with Catholicism ("I ain't Catholic."), technique 29. Thus the "formula" for this joke would be REL/43/21/29.

Exhibit 3.2: Basic Techniques and Popular Subjects of Humor

Basic Techniques		Popular Subjects	
1	absurdity	ADV	advertising
2	accident	AGR	agrarians
3	allusion	ANI	animals
4	analogy	ART	artists
5	before/after	BUS	businessmen
6	bombast	CEL	celebrities
7	burlesque	CHI	children
8	caricature (visual)	CLE	clergy
9	catalogue	COL	college students
10	chase scene	CON	convicts
11	coincidence	COW	cowboys
12	comparison	DOC	doctors
13	definition	DRU	drunks
14	disappointment	FAM	family life
15	eccentricity	FUN	funerals
16	embarrassment (escape from)	GEO	geographical areas
17	exaggeration, tall tales	INS	insane people
18	exposure	LAW	lawyers
19	facetiousness	LOV	love
20	grotesque	MAR	marriage
21	ignorance, gullibility	MIL	military
22	imitation	MOR	morons
23	impersonation	MOT	mothers-in-law
24	infantilism	NAT	nationalities
25	insults	NEW	newlyweds
26	irony	PAR	parents
27	literalness	POL	politics, politicians
28	mimicry	PSY	psychiatrists, psychologists
29	mistakes	REL	religion
30	misunderstanding	SAL	salesmen
31	parody	SEX	sex
32	puns	SOC	society types
33	repartee, outwitting	SPO	sports
34	repetition, pattern	WET	weather
35	reversal, getting even	WRI	writer
36	ridicule		
37	rigidity	Other subjects can be added as
38	sarcasm	needed	

```
┌─────────────────────────────────────────────────────┐
│              Exhibit 3.2  Continued                   │
│  39  satire                                           │
│  40  scale, size                                      │
│  41  slapstick                                        │
│  42  speed                                            │
│  43  stereotypes                                      │
│  44  theme and variation                              │
│  45  unmasking, revelation                            │
└─────────────────────────────────────────────────────┘
```

Find the formulas for the following jokes using the Comedy Calculator. Choose *one* subject and no more than *three* techniques when you analyze these jokes.

(a) During a rainstorm a man looks out of his office window and says, "It's raining cats and dogs." "I know," says a co-worker who has just come indoors. "I just stepped on a poodle."

(b) The doctor came out of the bedroom with a serious expression on his face. "I don't like the way your wife looks, Mr. Jones," he said. "Neither do I," replied Jones.

(c) On her deathbed, a beautiful actress burst into tears and said to her husband, "You've been so good to me and I've been so bad. I've been unfaithful more than a hundred times." "Don't excite yourself," said the husband. "Who do you think put the arsenic in your coffee?"

5. In this exercise we play with sound. We will use the "eye" sound as the focus of our attention and will write a story about an ophthalmologist (eye doctor) and his or her adventures. Here are some riddles with eye sounds:

Q. What does an ophthalmologist like best for dessert?

A. Ice cream.

Q. Where do ophthalmologists like to go on vacation?

A. Ireland.

In playing this game, do the following:

(a) Write 30 to 40 "eye" sounds. Do this by brainstorming. Don't reject any "eye" sounds while doing this.

(b) Write a story about an ophthalmologist that incorporates as many "eye" sounds in it as possible. Use your imagination. Deal with his/her travels, loves, adventures, and so on.

(c) Incorporate as many of the basic techniques of humor as you can into the story: exaggeration, absurdity, and others.

(d) If you can get "eye" sounds that are in the middle of a word or can find double or triple "eye" sounds, all the better.

(e) If you can find "eye" sounds in foreign languages, you get added points.

(f) Stretch sounds that are close to "eye" sounds, also.

(g) Find other sounds to play with and repeat this exercise in your journal. I have done drawings based on "cons," and there is a cartoon book based on "terns" (birds).

Although this is a silly exercise, after having written your stories, you will have created humor—using one of the most common techniques of humor, puns and wordplay. Try your hand at other techniques.

Being entirely honest with oneself is a good exercise. Only one idea of general value has occurred to me. I have found love of the mother and jealousy of the father in my own case too, and now believe it to be a general phenomenon of early childhood, even if it does not always occur so early as in children who have been made hysterics. . . . If that is the case, the gripping power of *Oedipus Rex*, in spite of all the rational objections to the inexorable fate that the story presupposes, becomes intelligible, and one can understand why later fate dramas were such failures. Our feelings rise against any arbitrary individual fate . . . but the Greek myth seizes on a compulsion which everyone recognizes because he has felt traces of it in himself. Every member of the audience was once a budding Oedipus in fantasy, and this dream-fulfillment played out in reality causes everyone to recoil in horror, with the full measure of repression which separates his infantile from his present state.

—Sigmund Freud, letter to Wilhelm Fliess, October 15, 1897

4

Journal Writing

In *Indiana Jones and the Last Crusade,* a journal kept by the elder Professor Jones plays a pivotal role. It has notes, drawings, and diagrams of crucial significance, and the leading characters in the film spend most of their energy trying to get their hands on this journal, for it contains information that is needed to find the lost temple and obtain the desired chalice.

Let me suggest that the senior Professor Jones was onto something important and that his journal keeping should be a model for all writers and researchers, for reasons that will be explained below.

The Difference Between Journals and Diaries

Keeping a journal is a subject that I can speak about with some authority, as I've been keeping one since 1954—and have written more than 50 journals in that time. The term *keeping* is very important because it suggests some kind of an obligation. You have to write in your journal regularly or it loses its value.

We should make a distinction here between a journal and a diary. A diary, as the term is generally used, is a record of private experiences that focuses upon personal matters, relationships, and that kind of thing. A journal, on the other hand, has a much different focus—ideas, thoughts, reflections, and speculations about various subjects. It may mention some "private" matters (it is impossible to avoid writing about one's feelings and activities), but the thrust of the journal should be ideas rather than personal matters.

A journal, from this point of view, is a kind of intellectual (and to some degree emotional) autobiography. It is a record of a person's ideas, thoughts, speculations, plans, and projects—

all of which are part of that "internal dialogue" we carry on with ourselves.

The Benefits of Keeping a Journal

What is important about journals is that the ideas we write about are not lost, as they often are when we "think about things" and get wonderful ideas but don't write them down. In addition, the process of writing about ideas leads to new ideas that pop into our heads, suddenly. The process of writing as one thinks is crucial, for the thinking, somehow, spurs our creative impulses, and we seem to gain access to our unconscious and dredge up notions and concepts we didn't know we had.

We can return to these ideas, later on, and develop them. I find that I often review my old journals and discover material that I can use in my various writing projects. Actually, all of my writing (including this book) has sprung from one or more of my journals. The idea for this book started in one journal. Then, in another journal, I started speculating about what such a book might be like, and in a third journal I made notes that I used in writing the various chapters.

Rules for Keeping a Journal

Everyone has a different way of working. I have a friend who writes all his books out in longhand. He gives this material to a secretary to type up. It is a much slower process than typing (and using ten fingers and a keyboard), but he's written more than 20 books and hundreds of articles, so his system works for him. I would like to suggest a number of rules or procedures that I have found useful in journal keeping. You may find them too restrictive or bothersome; what is important, in the final analysis, is that you keep a journal and write in it regularly. Everything else is unimportant.

Use a Bound Book for Your Journal. I keep my journals in bound black notebooks of the type that artists use for sketching. These notebooks are about five inches by eight inches and are blank.

It is important to use a bound book because the fact that it is bound gives it an element of permanence and prevents one from throwing pages away or adding pages after the fact. You can also carry it around with you and write in it in spare moments, if you wish. I ask my students to use bound laboratory notebooks—the same books that are used in science labs.

Number the Pages in Your Journal and Make an Index. This is crucial to maximize the value of your journal. You should devote a page or two to the index. Having an index enables you to access your notes—to see what you've written or add new material. I made an index on the last page of each of my journals. It is a chart in which I list page numbers and topics of interest. At times my journals deal with trivial matters and "fluff," so not every page is worth indexing. The page numbers record topics dealt with on that page (sometimes pages). Write on every line and both sides of every page, too.

Use Headlines to Highlight Topics. When I write, and decide to speculate on some subject, I generally indicate the topic by using all caps, to give it a kind of visual display. For example, suppose I decided to speculate on a television program that interested me. I would put the title of the show in all caps and then list my ideas about the show below. I would then indicate the page (or pages) in my index.

Use Diagrams, Charts, Lists, and Drawings. Journals don't have to be all writing. It is permissible (even desirable) also to make outlines, annotated lists, charts, and diagrams in which you play around with ideas, brainstorm, and speculate. This kind of thing enables you to see how ideas relate to one another and function as a personal form of infographics, which is a very useful way of conveying information. It is also a good idea to make little drawings from time to time, as they often prompt ideas and give your journals visual interest.

Ideally, then, your journal will consist of lines, even pages, of written text interspersed with pages (or parts of pages) in which there are lists, charts, and other kinds of infographics. If you are dealing with a big subject, you can set aside space for later ideas on it. You might also find it useful to divide pages vertically into halves, thirds, or quarters in some cases—when you have a big topic and want to be able to list ideas and do a great deal of thinking and outlining.

Date Each Day's Writing. This enables you to see what you were thinking when you were thinking it. You may not write in your journal every day, though it is a good idea to get in the habit of writing *something* in your journal daily, just to keep your mind working. Even ten minutes' worth of writing can often be beneficial, for it is the process of learning to think and write at the same time that is crucial. Something remarkable happens when you write in journals—the process often takes over and inhibitions (intellectual and otherwise) slip away and insights often occur, out of the blue.

Socrates said that thinking is "a dialogue we have with ourselves," and writing out this dialogue in journals is an effective way of saving this dialogue for later use.

Some of my students complain that they can't think of anything to write about in their journals if they are barred from writing about personal matters ("I've a crush on the guy/girl who sits next to me in chemistry") and feelings. My answer would be that any writing is better than no writing and that students should write about personal matters, if they wish to, or must, but that they keep trying to steer their writing away from personal matters. My own journals, I must confess, also have material in them that is not purely academic or intellectual. We cannot function purely on an intellectual basis, so a certain amount of writing about personal matters is acceptable.

Write in Ink. Pencil writing smudges and can be hard to read, so one should write in ink in journals.

Don't Write Assignments or Take Class Notes in Journals. Journals are meant to be records of ideas and speculations and should *not* be used for writing drafts of papers or taking class notes. You can, however, make outlines for papers in journals (an excellent use for them) and speculate about ideas and concepts learned in lectures.

All of these are suggestions offered on the basis of my 35 years of writing journals. These rules have evolved over the years; my first journals were less organized and structured—and less useful, I might add. Different persons will write journals different ways, to suit their own working habits. That's obvious. But keeping a journal is, let me suggest, a crucial matter for writers and students of writing. It is worth trying for a semester. (I started keeping a journal in 1954 at the suggestion of one of my teachers, Marguerite Young, at the University of Iowa Writers' Workshop.)

Ideas for Journal Keepers

Let me offer a number of suggestions for subjects or topics you might consider if you are having trouble thinking up things to write about. (Much of this trouble, I would suggest, comes from not being used to finding things to write about, from not being in the habit of being speculative. After a bit of practice, like anything else, it will be a lot easier.)

The Meanings of Concepts. Here you consider various concepts you come across in lectures or in reading. What is "existentialism"? What is meant by "the grotesque," or any of the other topics in the list of techniques of humor presented earlier, for example? What examples can you find for each? You can speculate about what concepts mean, how they are different from related concepts or concepts that are diametrically opposed to them. In the latter respect, you might make a chart listing the differences between a journal and a diary, between essays and dialogues, between eros (sexual love) and agape (nonsexual love), between the East Coast and the West Coast, and so on.

Projects You Are Working On. Do you have a term paper to write? What is its subject? How will you develop it? What research sources will you use? You might divide a page vertically into four columns and use each of column for a section of the paper or for a variety of purposes. Do you have an idea for a script for a situation comedy? You can list ideas on a page and try to get a clearer understanding of what the sitcom might be like. Were you assigned a documentary? You can speculate on it.

Reviews of Television Shows, Films, or Songs. Here you might list ideas or comments that come to your mind about some television show, film, song, or whatever. These ideas can be turned into an essay or a review, should you need (or wish) to do so.

Speculations About Why You Are Having Trouble Writing. This is permissible, too. As a writer, you can comment on any aspect of writing, including such matters as what your "style" of writing is, what is good and bad about your "style" of writing, how you hope to develop your "style" of writing, and other writers you like (and what, in particular, they do). You might also write about what you have written and what you hope to write about, ideas for articles, stories, plays, novels, commercials—you name it.

If you are writer, you must be interested in everything and always be alert for material to use. Everything should be grist for your mill and you must think a good deal about your work.

Exercise

1. Purchase a bound sketching notebook and number the pages, or purchase a laboratory notebook (which comes with the pages already numbered). Use either the first page or the last page for an index. You can give the journal a name if you wish, and a volume number (if you think you might like to keep journals regularly). If you are having trouble thinking of what to write about, consult the list of topics offered above.

JOYCE: You are an over-excited little man, with a need for self-expression far beyond the scope of your natural gifts. This is not discreditable. Neither does it make you an artist. An artist is a magician put among men to gratify—capriciously—their urge for immortality. The temples are built and brought down around him, continuously and contiguously, from Troy to the fields of Flanders. If there is any meaning in any of it, it is what survives as art, yes even in the celebration of tyrants, yes even in the celebration of nonentities. What now of the Trojan War if it had been passed over by the artist's touch? Dust. A forgotten expedition prompted by Greek merchants looking for new markets. A minor redistribution of broken pots. But it is we who stand enriched, by a tale of heroes, of a golden apple, a wooden horse, a face that launched a thousand ships—and above all, of Ulysses, the wanderer, the most human, the most complete of all heroes—husband, father, son, lover, farmer, soldier, pacifist, politician, inventor, and adventurer. . . . It is a theme so overwhelming that I am almost afraid to treat it. And yet I with my Dublin Odyssey will double that immortality.

—Tom Stoppard, *Travesties* (1975, p. 62)

5

Proscriptions

Thou shalt not pass in first drafts! That is a rule to follow always. There may be times when you are weak, when you are tempted to go out with your friends and get a pizza instead of revising and rewriting an assignment. Don't succumb. You will save money, you will avoid eating things that are bad for you, and you will sleep without a guilty conscience. This rule applies, also, if your friends invite you out to a health food restaurant to eat sprouts and tofu. Remember: Thou shalt not pass in first drafts.

You might say to yourself, "I'll get up early in the morning and write the assignment." And you may actually get up early the next morning and write the assignment. Believe me, it will be lousy. Don't kid yourself by telling yourself, "But I do my best work under pressure." You don't; except for a few geniuses like Mozart, artists need to revise their work over and over again. Some words of advice:

Do Not Get Discouraged. Writers, until they are established, often get rejection slips. As a friend of mine who is a successful writer put it, "Expect to get rejected. That's the norm. It is the acceptances that should surprise you." Getting rejected doesn't mean your work isn't good—though it doesn't mean it is good, either. What it means is that some editor doesn't like your work. It also doesn't mean that the editor doesn't like you. The same applies to professors, of course. They may give you poor grades; don't take them as attacks on you as a person.

Editors often reject works that are later published by other companies—works that win important prizes and make millions of dollars. From this we draw the moral that editors, producers, and so on don't know what they are doing! Except when they accept your work, that is—or a teacher gives you a good grade.

Don't Expect Everything You Write to Be Good. Great novelists sometimes write lousy novels, just as great directors make lousy films. You can't expect to succeed all the time. In fact, you should count yourself lucky if even a small percentage of what you write is good. What is important is that you learn from your mistakes and don't keep repeating them.

Don't Stop Experimenting. This is a very difficult rule for creative artists of all kinds. In certain respects, an early success can be devastating, because you may be tempted to keep on doing the same thing, over and over again—lest you "fail." What happens, then, is you die as far as your creativity is concerned. That's why it isn't always good to succeed too early, because you (like many others) can be "destroyed by success." Woody Allen has said that he is willing to try new things and fail, because that shows that he is continuing to grow. It is a hard lesson to learn, but if you find you are repeating yourself over and over again, it means you've stopped trying new things. So if you don't fail from time to time, something's wrong.

Don't Write Too Much at One Time. It's a good deal better to write three hours a day, five days a week, than eight hours a day for two days. If you really tire yourself, you'll spend the rest of the week recuperating. In emergencies, of course, long sessions are understandable, though you probably won't be operating at peak efficiency. If you can learn to be disciplined, organize your time, and structure your workdays, you can avoid this kind of thing. Whenever you try to do too much, you end up with too little. That's one of life's ironies.

Don't Expect Anyone to Teach You How to Write! That's a strange statement in a book on writing. What I mean is that writing is a very personal matter and you will have to take responsibility and learn how to write on your own. In this book I can give you hints, I can offer suggestions, I can point out mistakes writers make—but in the final analysis, you have to teach yourself how to write, just as you have to teach yourself how to do all kinds of other things.

Sometimes I wonder whether we can teach people anything. What we can do, it seems, is facilitate learning. Teaching puts too much responsibility on the teacher and not enough on the student, which is why I like the notion that learning is the issue, not teaching. But I've never had an education course, so what do I know?

In Part I, I have offered information about writing styles and ideas about comedy writing and a number of rules about various formats and things like that. I also provided scripts for the various kinds of writing discussed in the book.

I can show you the steps, to return to our dancing analogy, but I can't turn you into a dancer. Nobody could turn Fred Astaire into a great dancer except one person—Fred Astaire. Of course, it helps if you have a good teacher, and I believe that the following chapters will be useful to you in a number of ways, but in the arts—and writing is an art—the main impetus has to come from within the artist, which means from within you.

PART II

Scripts

Now the serpent was more subtle than any beast of the field which the Lord God had made.

And he said unto the woman,

"Yea, hath God said, 'Ye shall not eat of every tree of the garden'?"

And the woman said unto the serpent,

"We may eat of the fruit of the trees of the garden; but of the fruit of the tree which is in the midst of the Garden, God hath said, 'Ye shall not eat of it, neither shall ye touch it, lest ye die.' "

And the serpent said unto the woman,

"Ye shall not surely die: for God doth know that in the day ye eat thereof, then your eyes shall be opened, and ye shall be as gods, knowing good and evil."

And when the woman saw that the tree was good for food, and that it was pleasant to the eyes, and a tree to be desired to make one wise, she took of the fruit thereof, and did eat, and gave also unto her husband with her; and he did eat. And the eyes of them both were opened. . . .

And the Lord God said unto the woman,

"What is this that thou hast done?"

And the woman said, "The serpent beguiled me, and I did eat."

—Genesis

6

Commercials

Commercials are the most important kind of television *text* (a term often used for a film, radio, or television show). In the United States, radio and television are private industries, and they run on the money generated by selling time for commercials. What radio and television stations must deliver to manufacturers and others selling products and services, then, is an audience. Not just any audience, either. If you are paying large amounts of money to air a commercial for an expensive car, for example, you want an audience made of people who buy expensive cars. A gigantic audience full of poor people is of no value. So it isn't the size of the audience but the nature of the audience that is crucial.

Let me offer a number of considerations that must be kept in mind when one is writing commercials, in general. Later on we will distinguish between radio and television commercials.

Methods Used in All Advertising

The term *advertising* covers all messages used to sell products, services, individuals (politicians), or ideas. Conventionally we use the term *advertisement* for print media and *commercial* for broadcast media.

Attract Attention. Somehow you must get the attention of your desired audience. This is a problem because most people do other things while they "watch" television or "listen" to the radio. They may be eating or reading a magazine or knitting or working. People generally do not give radio and television undivided attention. There is also the matter of a sense people have that when commercials come on they should not pay attention and that it's a good time to do other things (such as go to the bathroom or get a snack from the kitchen).

There is also the matter of "clutter," the chaos generated by the large number of commercials a viewer or listener is exposed to in a given period. Thus attracting attention isn't as easy as it might sound.

Stimulate Desire. Somehow, through logic or emotion, you must get members of your audience to *desire* (a stronger term than *want*—with sexual overtones) your product or service. There are numerous ways this can be done, but all have problems. If, for example, you use a beautiful woman to sell a product, people may not pay any attention to the product because they are "turned on" by the woman. I will discuss a number of techniques that can be used to "sell" products shortly.

Generate Action. Find a way to get people to act on their decision to purchase your product. Get them to call a number and order it, or decide to purchase it the next time they are at the store, or do something else, other than just filing the information away in their heads. This is why emotion is so important in advertising. People often believe that they are swayed only by logic (and what they find in *Consumer Reports*), but this is not true. We know, for example, that something like two-thirds of the purchases made in supermarkets are spur-of-the-moment decisions.

These are the most general principles on which all advertising relies. You can't sell people something if you don't have their attention and don't get them to want what you are selling and don't get them to act (or even decide to act) and purchase your product. It's how you do this that is the problem, which is why advertising agencies are always conducting test campaigns before they launch national ones. (As one advertising agency person supposedly put it, "Let's run it up the flagpole and see if anyone salutes.")

In their desperate pursuit of audiences and sales, advertising agencies (and the clients they work for) have been known, in some instances, to act in questionable or even immoral ways. A famous case of this was one commercial for soup in which the advertising agency had placed marbles in the bowl, which kept the ingredients at the top, so the soup looked much heartier than it actually was. There are also questions about the roles women are given and what some critics consider to be a debasing of female sexuality (and now male sexuality as well) to sell goods and services.

Selling Appeals for Products and Services

Here we move from the general to the specific and focus our attention on particular products and services. What is distinctive or special about the product or service—if anything is at all? (In the case of cigarettes, soap powder, and gasoline, for example, the products are virtually identical, so you don't sell the product itself but something associated with the product, such as "the West" and "freedom," or something vague, like "taste.")

How do you position your product or service? What appeals do you offer? Do you try to reach this market in terms of its demographics (age, income, sex, marital status) or psychographics (psychological makeup)? One complicating factor is that people in various groups frequently don't always act the way you expect them to act or the way they are "supposed" to act. How do you factor this into the equation?

What follows is a list of some of the most common ways of appealing to audiences and influencing them to purchase a product or service. (It is hard to know whether politicians are best seen as selling a product, themselves, or a service, their intellect and power. In one campaign, Nelson Rockefeller was running for reelection as governor of New York, but was very unpopular. He was never shown on the screen—only drug addicts, clogged highways, and other such problems were shown. The person behind the campaign said that he didn't think of Rockefeller as a person but that he sold him the way he would sell soap.)

It is not unusual for a number of these appeals to be used together.

Anxiety. Here we generate some anxiety in people ("You stink, which is why, though you are beautiful, men avoid you") and then offer a solution ("Use our underarm deodorant and you'll find Mr. Wonderful in no time at all"). We then show our heroine, once scorned by men, using our product, and attracting a handsome man.

Benefits Stated. This appeal is more logical; it shows people the various benefits they can expect to get from purchasing a given product or service. Sometimes, direct comparisons are made and charts are offered showing how product X is less expensive, longer lasting, and more powerful than product Y. All advertising suggests that one benefits from buying a given product or service, but in the benefits appeal, the focus is directly on the benefits and the method used is, perhaps, more logical than emotional.

Humor. Humor is a controversial matter in advertising. Some advertisers believe it works magic and others feel it demeans what it sells and distracts attention from a product or service. Others believe that giving people pleasure through humor puts them in a more receptive frame of mind. In recent years I think humor has become more valued as a way of appealing to people, but good humor is difficult to write. And one must be always careful about offending people.

Testimonials. Here someone (a celebrity or an ordinary person) tells us how wonderful the product or service is and how much he or she likes it, and urges us to purchase it. This approach may be looked upon as an attempt to simulate word-of-mouth advice, which is a very powerful way of getting people to act. If we know someone who speaks from personal experience, is very positive about some product or service, and has nothing to gain by telling us about it, we are much more likely to try it than we are because we've seen a commercial. It also plays upon a desire many people have to imitate (by consumption) sports heroes, movie stars, and other kinds of celebrities.

Demonstrations. A demonstration is used to show how something works or what benefits we will get from purchasing a product or a service. It is a simulation designed to give us a sense of what the actual experience of using a product or service is like. This appeal depends on our notion that "seeing is believing." Sometimes, of course, that isn't the case and we are duped. What you see isn't always what you get: Many blondes are really brunettes, men with bushy heads of hair are bald, and doctors who speak to us so knowledgeably turn out to be impostors.

Indirect Appeals. These might be called "life-style" appeals, also. They are a form of the "soft sell." We are shown people who attract us or scenes that interest us and that generate certain feelings about life. On television these commercials are often quite arty and use many avant-garde video techniques. Then, at the end, the name of the product is shown. The advertiser is telling us that we are so sophisticated that we don't need to be given a "hard sell," in which the name of the product or service is repeated endlessly and we are urged, directly, and often abrasively, to purchase or do something.

Join the Crowd. Here the appeal is to the herd instinct—to our desire to be liked and to be like other people. If we can be convinced that everyone is doing something, and we don't want to either stand out or be last in line for something good, we are likely to respond the "proper" way to a commercial. This can be reversed with "snob" appeals—appeals that aim to make us want to use products and services that most people can't afford or are too common or unimaginative to appreciate.

This list offers some of the more commonly used appeals found in commercials. You may think of others that fit you and your writing style better and want to use them. In all cases, however, you must make sure the appeals you use "fit" your product.

Scriptwriting Techniques

Now it is time to turn our attention to some of the basic categories of commercials. They are often mixed together.

The Scenario. This term describes a "scene" (as in a play) in which various characters interact with one another. The product or service generally plays an important role in this scenario and is promoted by one character or another. Sound effects and music may be used in the scenario. We are members of the audience who are observing something going on, a "slice of life" in some cases.

The Direct Pitch. In this category, someone talks directly to us (the audience), employing (in the case of television) as much body language, sex appeal, and facial expression as possible to convince us to use a product or service. In some cases, this pitch person functions as a narrator for a scenario or appears in one and then makes a pitch to us.

In radio, on the other hand, many commercials are simply read, or someone, an announcer or talk-show host or disk jockey, reads a closing statement before or after (or before *and* after) a recorded commercial is played: a jingle, a testimonial, a scenario.

Jingles. This is a technique that uses music and rhyme to sell us a product. Many jingles are quite catchy and very memorable. (Young children often know dozens of them.) The theory: If we remember the jingle and thus the product or service, we are more likely to purchase it than if we don't. Jingles can be added to scenarios or direct pitches.

These three categories can be summarized as follows: Show them; talk to them; sing to them. It is how you do so and what appeals you make in your commercial that make the difference. The final matter to deal with involves the difference between radio and television commercials, which will be discussed below.

Radio Commercials

As the Stan Freberg commercial discussed in Chapter 2 shows, radio is an auditory medium that can take advantage of our ability to imagine all kinds of incredible things. So you can create "situations" or "scenarios" in radio that are impossible (or, in some cases, too expensive) to do in television. On the other hand, since we generally don't give undivided attention

---

Exhibit 6.1: Sample Radio Commercial

```
        The Cove at Edgewater Isle
        :60 Radio "Crisis"
SFX:    SHORT BURST OF PHONE BEEP
SHE:    Home Buyers Hotline, I'm Joy. . . .
HE:     I'm Graham. I'm angry. I'm frustrated.
SHE:    I understand, Graham. Share it with me.
HE:     Me, my wife, we're . . . first time buyers.
SHE:    Ooh, how depressing . . .
HE:     With good taste.
SHE:    Ooh, how awful. . . .
HE:     And jobs in the city.
SHE:    Ooh, how sickening . . . Did you talk to
        the agents?
HE:     Of course. We said around 130 . . . they
        said around Modesto.
HE:     We mentioned a quiet cul-de-sac . . . they
        had a dead end in Colma.
HE:     We asked for a view of the water . . .
        they took us to Alviso in the rain.
SHE:    Listen Graham, hang up the phone, pick up
        your wife and whisper these words in her
        ear: The Cove.
HE:     (Whisper) The Cove.
SHE:    At Edgewater Isle . . .
VO:     The Cove at Edgewater Isle (in San Mateo).
        Quiet (affordable) condominiums on a se-
        cluded lagoon, starting at just 132,000.
        With five elegant floor plans (loft space)
        docking facilities (and water views). All
        with comfortable financing and commute.

        The Cove at Edgewater Isle (toward the San
        Mateo Bridge). You can come for the com-
        fort, or the cove itself, but you'll come
        to stay.
```

Used by permission of Johnson & Joyce.

to radio when we listen to it, and since it is relatively hard to follow and remember what we hear, radio scripts must be relatively simple, with short bits of dialogue by the various characters. Simple announcements also have to be written carefully, keeping in mind the suggestions made earlier about spoken language.

Radio is a "local" and highly segmented medium, so you must consider the demographics and psychographics (as well as the values and life-styles) of the station's audience. But this segmentation is useful, too, because it allows you to focus on very specific audiences for your commercials (teenagers, senior citizens, suburban housewives, and so on). Radio commercials are inexpensive to produce (relative to television commercials) and it is easy to create a number of different commercials that can be pinpointed at different target audiences.

Television Commercials. Aside from cheapie television commercials made by the owners of automobile dealers and appliance stores, the average commercial costs in the vicinity of $200,000 to make and a great deal more to air on television stations. This does not mean that television commercials are always more expensive than print advertising. Advertisers measure their expenses on a "cost per thousand" (or CPM) basis, so a television commercial that costs $150,000 to make and air but that reaches 50 million people is actually much less expensive than a print advertisement that costs $15,000 and reaches 250,000 people. It is the CPM that is the basic measure, as well as the demographics of the people reached.

Because many television commercials are meant for national as well as local audiences, they cannot be as narrowly focused as radio commercials. Television is a visual as well as auditory medium, and makes use of the power of images to affect our emotions and stimulate desire in people. Because of the large costs involved in producing and purchasing time for airing commercials, advertising agencies spend a great deal of time and money in research.

There is always tension in agencies between the researchers, who have all kinds of statistics about projected audiences for commercials, and the "creative" people—the artists and copywriters—who write the scripts and direct the production of commercials. Another factor involves the taste, imagination, and attitudes of the people who manufacture the products or run the companies offering services being sold. "He who pays

Exhibit 6.2: Sample Television Commercial

OPEN ON WARRIOR PLAYERS IN ASPHALT
JUNGLE SETTING, TO SUGGEST GETTING
BACK TO TOUGH STREET PLAYING ROOTS.
SFX: DRIBBLING STOPS. CU OF PLAYER.

First player: Some people think . . .

SFX: WHOOSH & POP OF BASKETBALL
FLYING THROUGH AIR AND BEING
CAUGHT. IT'S SUDDENLY PASSED TO
ANOTHER PLAYER WHO PICKS UP THE
ACTION.

Second Player: We haven't got what
it takes . . .

FAST PACED PASSING CONTINUES
SFX: WHOOSH & POP OF BASKETBALL

Third Player: To bounce back . . .

PLAYER PAUSES FOR A DRAMATIC MOMENT
THAN PASSES. OFF CAMERA, A FOURTH
PLAYER CONTINUES TALKIN TOUGH.
SFX: WHOOSH & POP OF BASKETBALL

Fourth Player: We've just got one
                thing . . .

(continued)

Exhibit 6.2 Continued

FINAL PLAYER DOES A BIG ROLL WITH
HIS WRIST TO BEGIN DRIBBLING

Fourth player: tO SAY TO YOU . . .

MEDIUM SHOT OF BASKETBALL AS IT
TRAVELS FULL SPEED AT THE GROUND.
SFX: WHOOOOSH!

BASKETBALL EXPLODES ON IMPACT.
SFX:CRASH

VO: It's Payback Time

the piper calls the tune," and in the final analysis, the company doing the advertising must be satisfied. And the commercials must sell.

Scripts for television commercials use the standard divided page format, with the video on the left and the audio on the right. These scripts usually are accompanied by a storyboard, which shows a number of the most important images (frames) from a commercial, as envisioned by the writers and artists creating the commercial.

Exhibit 6.3: Sample Television Commercial

CORPORATE OFFICE. DEL
HAS CALLED IN HELEN
TO DISCUSS BUDGET
MATTERS. A THICK
REPORT IS
OPEN ON HIS DESK.

DEL:
Sit down, Helen. I
wanted to ask you
about this line
item.
[POINTS OUT SECTION
OF REPORT.] We
never budgeted for
this.

ECU HELEN.

HELEN:
Those are
computer costs.

Exhibit 6.3   Continued

ECU DEL.

DEL:
But Helen, we paid
for those systems
last quarter.

<u>HELEN:</u>
Those are training
costs.

<u>DEL:</u>
Training . . .
costs more than the
computers them-
selves? Memphis
doesn't show these
costs.

ECU HELEN.

Exhibit 6.3   Continued

ECU DEL.

DEL:
So?

ECU HELEN.

HELEN:
Apparently, with
their computers
. . . their people
can, uh, train
themselves

FADE TO BLACK.

Exercises

1. Write a 150-word radio script for the product described below. *Note that this exercise is in terms of words rather than seconds.* Bring your script to within five words, under or over, of the assigned number. Please keep in mind all of the considerations described in this chapter. These scripts should be scenarios with at least three characters and full production values.

> GOLD STAR TEA
> expensive Darjeeling leaves
> hand-picked in India from first pickings
> aged five years
> winner of three gold stars at international competitions
> smooth, smoky taste

2. Write comedy radio scripts for Gold Star Tea using the following dialects:

> upper-class English
> Russian

Remember that you must deal with commonly held stereotypes of these groups and with the national character and various aspects of each of these cultures.

3. Write 150-word radio commercials (scenarios with full production values) for the following products:

> (a) OAT DELIGHTS
> contains nutritious oat bran
> helps decrease cholesterol
> crunchy flakes, don't get soggy in milk
> delicious oat taste
> no sugar or salt
> can be used to make oat bran muffins; recipe on box

> (b) PANHARMONIC Z-30 BOOM BOX
> two four-inch speakers
> soft release
> powerful AM/FM reception
> light—only three pounds
> automatic turn off
> long battery life

4. Write a 100-word (words of dialogue) television script for one of the products described below.

> (a) LEVI'S TRUE-BLUES (DENIM PANTS)
> all cotton
> reinforced seams

    strong 14-ounce denim
    European "tight-fit" tailoring
    prewashed
    tops in style and comfort

(b) NATIONAL EDITION OF THE *NEW YORK TIMES*
    authoritative yet lively writing
    newspaper of record
    most prestigious newspaper in the United States
    three sections: news, living arts, business
    first three months half price for new subscribers
    call toll free to subscribe—1 (800) 631-2500

(c) PREDATOR PERFUME, BY COUNT IGOR MALINOWSKI
    $50 an ounce
    "For lovers who won't take no for an answer"
    blended in France from rarest flowers
    sophisticated, elegant scent
    sold only in finest shops
    comes in beautiful cut-crystal container

Remember that you need not use all of the attributes of a product in making your commercials. Be imaginative. Avoid dull, prosaic scenarios and dialogue. Try to combine an interesting, unusual, fresh concept with lively dialogue. Also remember to think visually: consider the kinds of shots you will use, the cutting, and camera angles you might use.

Make sure you have a variety of different kinds of shots, otherwise the commercial will be visually boring. Make sure, also, that you check the specifications and follow them carefully. Make sure that your commercial has "selling" power.

Give every man thy ear, but few thy voice;
Take each man's censure, but reserve thy judgment.
Costly thy habit as thy purse can buy,
But not expressed in fancy; rich not gaudy,
For the apparel oft proclaims the man,
And they in France of the best rank and station
Are of a most select and generous chief in that.
Neither a borrower nor a lender be,
For loan oft loses both itself and friend,
And borrowing dulls th' edge of husbandry.
This above all, to thine own self be true,
And it must follow as the night the day
Thou canst not then be false to any man.

—William Shakespeare, *Hamlet*,
Act I, Scene 3

7

Features

It's hard to explain exactly what a feature is. Perhaps it will be more useful to discuss some of the basic attributes of features as a way of generating an understanding of what features are and what they do.

Features Are Not News Reports. They are not news reports, in which the primary effort is to offer an accurate picture of some current event. But features are often about events—and one of the more common kind of features, the *anniversary feature*, returns to some event from the past to remind us about it and put it in perspective.

Features Are Often Stories. That means we must give them a form or structure that listeners will find interesting. In anniversary features, we do this by focusing upon such things as the excitement generated by the original event or the important consequences of the event. Although features are generally seen as allied to "news" (as contrasted with fictional stories, for instance), they should be interesting and entertaining.

In some cases, a news story can be turned into a feature story by interviewing the various people involved and getting their different perspectives on the matter. One can also create a fictional "drama" based on the news story, if it lends itself to that kind of thing. The point is, features allow all kinds of creativity and inventiveness.

Features Are Personal. It is common to interview people involved, one way or another, with the event being "featured." One might interview participants in the event, bystanders, and experts on the subject, as well as use material taped when the original event took place (if it is available). I can still recall an

105

anniversary story that I heard years ago. It was about the burning of the Hindenburg zeppelin and the tragic loss of life in that holocaust. It used a sound bite of an announcer, in tears, describing what happened as the Hindenburg suddenly burst into flames. The main thing in an anniversary feature is to provide listeners with a sense of what an event was like and what its impact has been.

The element of personality plays an important role in features. Whereas a news report deals with people and events in as factual and objective a manner as possible, a feature emphasizes the human interest side of things. Some features are commentaries that have nothing to do with anything of news significance, and merely explore some subject of interest to the person who makes the feature: A feature can be on people, ideas, cultural matters, oddball events, or whatever. Many features contain a mix of interviews, narration about background information, tapes of past actualities (material that has been recorded), and whatever else can be used to give the feature impact and presence.

Features Are Short. In radio, features generally run between 2 and 3 minutes long. We can see that a feature can be very close to being a short documentary. In television, we have mini-documentaries, which run from 10 to 15 minutes (as on *60 Minutes*, for example), and standard documentaries, which generally run for an hour (or even several hours in certain cases). In radio, we find many features on National Public Radio's news shows, which are very free form and allow people who create features much more time than they would get on commercial radio. Exhibit 7.1 presents an example of a radio feature that was originally broadcast on station KQED-FM, in Northern California (used by permission of Nate Shoehalter).

Exhibit 7.1: Redwoods

I suppose everyone remembers the first time he entered a redwood forest. For me, a displaced Easterner, it was a religious experience. The quiet, dark, cool awesomeness of the trees was unforgettable.

The fossil history of these trees goes back several millions of years; over the millennia changes have taken place and now the *Sequoia sempervirens* is restricted to a narrow area along the West Coast.

What strikes one is the lack of other plant species in the redwoods. Botanists at the Berkeley Botanical Garden tell us that there are sword ferns, redwood sorrel, the inside-out flower, and a trailing saxifrage under the canopy. There are also shrubs—the evergreen huckleberry, California bay rose, and wax myrtle. But surprisingly few other plants.

The Botanical Garden in Berkeley, where we live, has two areas where you can see some of these long-lived species—the five-acre Mather Red-Wood Grove and the Redwood Circle.

Why are these trees restricted to this narrow strip of the West Coast? Well, we have a moderate climate, summer fog that contributes about ten inches of equivalent rain during the summer, floods— the redwoods can tolerate silt burial by floods on a 30- to 60-year cyclical basis. The redwoods have a thick, spongy, fibrous bark which is fire resistant and insulates the living cells in the tree. Incidentally, the silt and the fire play important roles in creating conditions for redwood seed germination and eliminating potential tree competition.

On a sad note—the director of the University of California Berkeley Botanical Garden informs us that . . . "the Coast redwood had a much wider distribution in the geological past than it does at present and should be considered a species that is on its way out in an evolutionary sense."

We don't advocate that you rush out to see the trees, but when you do you will be seeing something that future generations may never have a chance to enjoy. In the meantime we can see and take pleasure in these immense imposing plants and remember when we first saw them.

I'm Nate Shoehalter for *Where We Live.*

Exercise

1. Prepare a radio anniversary feature. In this assignment you will deal with an event of historical importance and "bring it to life" in a 350-word (words of dialogue, that is) script. Please do the following for the assignment:

Do research. Base the feature on research and the use of a number of authoritative sources. You may consider printed material found in the library as being the equivalent of oral interviews. That is, written material will be assumed to be "interviews" and can be used as dialogue, as if it has been spoken by the writer, in your script. If someone has written an essay in which he says, "Punk is turning our kids into monsters," you can create dialogue using the writer as an interviewee, and have him say that.

Pick an event of some significance. For this anniversary feature, you should deal with some socially, politically, or historically important event. You can assume, for purposes of this exercise, that the feature will be aired on some anniversary of the event. It should have taken place at least one year earlier.

Consider the structure of your feature. Make sure your anniversary feature is entertaining and factually correct. Your feature should have an opening that will catch people's attention, should develop logically, and should have a strong ending. Don't stop writing when you reach the word limit for the assignment and leave your listeners "hanging in midair."

Do not write a historical feature. The focus of your feature should not be on the history of the subject you choose (that is, change over time), but on the subject's meaning and symbolic significance. Some questions you might consider include these: What does the event mean? What does it reflect about society, and about people? What impact has it had? What lessons can we learn from it?

Use actors, actresses, a narrator, sound effects, and music. This anniversary feature is not meant to be a single-voice narrated feature, but should be what I've called a "scenario," involving actors and actresses, dialogue, and the other attributes of a typical radio script. It should be

written in the conventional two-column radio script
format.

Submit your documentation. Attach duplicated copies of the
articles you used in researching this script and highlight the material from these articles that you used as
dialogue.

In the social production which men carry on they enter into definite relations that are indispensable and independent of their will; these relations of production correspond to a definite state of development of their material powers of production. The totality of these relations of production constitutes the economic structure of society—the real foundation, on which legal and political superstructures arise and to which definite forms of social consciousness correspond. The mode of production of material life determines the general character of the social, political and spiritual processes of life. It is not the consciousness of men that determines their being, but, on the contrary, their social being determines their consciousness.

—Karl Marx, *Preface to a Contribution to the Critique of Political Economy*

8

Documentaries

The documentary is one of the most common and most important genres in radio and television (and film, as well). We are all interested in life around us—and it is from documentaries that we learn about everything from the amazing adventures some courageous souls have experienced to the remarkable triumphs of our scientists, from the secrets of nature (and animal life) to the problems of our inner cities.

Although we are all familiar with documentaries and have a sense of what documentaries are, defining them is quite a problem.

What Is a Documentary?

Let me offer a few of the numerous definitions that have been offered of this term, which was first used by a distinguished filmmaker, John Grierson, in an unsigned review of a film by Robert Flaherty, *Moana*. Grierson wrote, "*Moana* being a visual account of events in the daily life of a Polynesian youth and his family, has documentary value" (quoted in Edmonds, 1974).

Documentaries are nonfiction. In this definition, a simple division is made between fiction and nonfiction, and anything that is nonfiction is understood as being a documentary. This definition is so broad that it is relatively useless. When a company makes a training video or a professor records a lecture, we have, according to this definition, documentaries.

The definition is helpful in that it does suggest we are dealing with "reality" (whatever that is) as contrasted with made-up stories. But what if one uses fiction, in scenes, to dramatize what life was really like in earlier periods? Or what about the development of a new mixed genre, docudrama, which

111

provides fictional accounts of "real" events? Keeping the problems of the fiction/nonfiction division in mind, let's move on to other definitions.

Documentaries involve the "creative treatment of actuality." This understanding of the term, offered by Grierson, also has problems: What is meant by "creative" and what is meant by "actuality"? In a later statement, Grierson changed the term *treatment* to *interpretation*, so documentaries were seen as "the creative interpretation of actuality." This definition merely adds one more vague term to the others listed above. How far, we may ask, does "interpretation" allow a documentary maker to go? Is a documentary supposed to be "objective" and reflect the world as accurately as the documentary maker can do so, or can "subjective" (personal, ideological) works also be considered to be documentaries?

Documentaries are current history, because they deal with how people live, what they want, how they try to get it. This definition, by the distinguished French documentary maker Jean Rouch, suggests the objective goal of the documentary, but says nothing about how one tries to reach this goal.

Documentaries involve all methods of recording any aspect of reality. This is the essence of the statement of the World Union of Documentary Film Makers, made in 1948. A more complete definition is offered: Documentaries include

> all methods of recording on celluloid any aspect of reality interpreted either by factual shooting or by sincere and justifiable reconstruction, so as to appeal either to reason or emotion, for the purpose of stimulating the desire for, and the widening of, human knowledge and understanding, and of truthfully posing problems and their solutions in the spheres of economics, culture and human relations.

This definition is also troublesome. Are documentary makers supposed to "record" reality or "impose their view" of reality upon us? It is obvious from looking at all the different definitions that have been discussed that it is extremely difficult to define (in the sense of "limit") documentaries. From all of these definitions, we do come away with certain understandings, however. Documentaries are nonfiction, they focus upon real people (as contrasted with invented or imaginary characters) and upon life around us, and they aim to be "truthful" in the way they reflect and interpret reality.

As I mentioned earlier, some documentaries are journalistic and follow a logical and linear thread, based essentially on cause and effect. Others are thematic and have different purposes—exploring some subject from various perspectives, following a different logic, using a structure that is closer to what we know as stream of consciousness. We might see two polarities here—journalism and art. One focuses on reflecting reality (a mirror) while the other "creates" and projects reality (a lamp). Let me offer another definition that will be useful for our particular purposes.

Documentaries are research reports made using sound and images. This is important because it suggests that scripts for documentaries might be used, in certain cases, as alternatives to the more traditional research papers assigned in courses. Documentaries are always based on research. It is only the method of presentation of one's findings—in the form of a script rather than a long essay—that is different.

Truth Versus Veracity

In *About Documentary: Anthropology on Film* (1974), documentary maker Robert Edmonds makes a distinction between *truth* and *veracity*. He writes, discussing two opposing views of the Vietnam War made with the same newsreel footage:

> The same newsreel footage, pictures of things which actually happened, can, it appears, be used to express opposite interpretations of the same events. . . . Film shots, like words, take their meaning from the other words in the sentences in which they are used. Just as a word is neither subject nor object until it occurs in a sentence, so a film shot is "alienated" from meaning until it is edited into a filmic sentence. (p. 17)

This is because meaning is not based on "facts" but on relationships, and by altering "facts" we can distort relationships. In other words, in documentaries (and essays as well), it is possible to "stack the deck" and, by filming (or citing) only selected instances, lead people astray. The camera records truthfully, but only what it is pointed at, so television reportage (and photographs and all visual images) can be used to distort matters, and to give "veracity" but not "truth."

Should Documentaries Be Used to Persuade?

There is a great deal of controversy over this question. Should documentaries try to be as objective as possible (and function as mirrors, so to speak), or should they advocate things and try to persuade people (and function as lamps, projecting a view of reality)? If you believe it is acceptable for documentaries to persuade, how do you prevent them from becoming instruments of propaganda?

It is impossible, of course, for any video or film report to be purely objective. There is always an element of selection and interpretation that takes place, which means that pure objectivity is impossible. The question is how far one goes in trying to be objective in contrast to taking a position and trying to influence people's opinions directly. For some people, the "emotive" impact is what is critical; they define documentaries as works (of nonfiction) that affect people, that "move" them.

We must also remember that a documentary is not a news story, per se (about events that are happening in the immediate present). The documentary must have dramatic appeal, should develop and reveal character, should have conflict and excitement, and should offer insights and revelations about people and the world about us. Some documentaries are historical and are based on compilations, but they also must be interesting and capable of holding an audience's attention.

Being a documentary maker is one of the most interesting and exciting careers a person might have. It offers a person the opportunity to exercise his or her creative talents (in researching and writing as well as taping or filming and editing), to inform people and entertain them, and, in many cases, to do something constructive for people and society in general.

Techniques to Use in Documentaries

The format for documentaries has already been described, in Chapter 2, along with material on camera shots and angles and related considerations. A number of devices that can be used in documentaries are described below.

Narrators. Documentaries often use a narrator to tie program elements together and give viewers a sense of things. Narration should not be overused. The documentary should be carried by the interviewees and by film or video of significant events. In other words, the documentary should *show* (rather than tell, through the narrator) viewers what they are to get from seeing the documentary. You must decide how the narrator is to be portrayed—if, that is, you are using one.

Voice-Overs or Tracks. Here we have a voice, either the narrator's or an interviewee's, discussing something that is being shown on the screen. Voice-overs should be used with discretion—to carry the action forward or to make some kind of an important point.

Dialogue. The documentary script is generally a combination of narration and dialogue. (You don't get much dialogue from the lead characters in nature documentaries.) The dialogue must be relevant and interesting and should generate dramatic excitement.

On-the-Scene Events. In documentaries, we use actualities, which can be defined as events that are filmed or videotaped as they occur. This involves everything from old newsreel footage to material documentary makers record themselves.

Staged Scenarios. Here we refer to re-creations, sometimes with actors and actresses, of a significant event. There is controversy among visual anthropologists over whether it is acceptable to stage rituals and similar matters so they can be recorded. In the same vein, some documentary makers do not consider staged re-creations to be acceptable for documentaries.

Cinema Verité and Direct Cinema. James Monaco explains the difference between these two approaches to making films in his book *How to Read a Film* (1977):

> The principal theory of Direct Cinema was that the filmmakers not involve themselves in the action. Gone were the well-phrased narrations of earlier documentaries. The camera was all-seeing: hundreds of hours of film were shot in order to capture a sense of the reality of the subject. Frederick Wiseman, trained as a lawyer, brought this technique to perfection in a remarkable series of studies of institutions for Public Television, among them *Titicut Follies* (1967, about a mental institution), *High School* (1968). . . .
>
> In France during the sixties, a parallel style of new documentary was developing. Called "cinéma vérité," it differed from direct cinema in that it admitted that the presence of the camera made a difference and indeed traded on that fact. *Chronicle d'un ete* (1960), by anthropologist Jean Rouch and sociologist Edgar Morin, was the first and still classic example of cinéma vérité. (p. 266)

Both of these techniques use the camera to capture reality, but they differ in terms of the role the camera plays and in the editing. Cinema verité tries to capture reality directly and doesn't involve the kind of editing we find in direct cinema. There is no music used in cinema verité and only natural sound is used. (A number of critics, I might add, consider the two styles to be identical.) These techniques were made possible by the development of lightweight cameras and sound recording, which gave documentary makers great mobility.

Interviews. The interview is one of the basic components of a documentary. Because there are usually many different points of view on any given topic, interviews of people with different perspectives on a given subject can be used to generate an element of conflict and excitement in a documentary. One must be careful not to "edit" the interview so that the point of view of the person being interviewed has been distorted, however.

Structure. You must decide on how you wish to structure the documentary—whether you use a linear or stream-of-consciousness (to cite the two extremes) form of organization. In many cases the subject of the documentary "suggests" the structure. In other cases, the style of a documentary maker shapes the way a documentary is structured.

Voice. Voice can be thought of as involving the tone documentary makers employ in their work—the personal attitudes that are shown in the way a given documentary is shot, edited, and structured. We might think of voice as what is distinctive about a documentary maker's style. A great deal depends on the intention of the documentary makers. Are they primarily interested in reflecting reality as accurately as they can or are they interested in making works that are propaganda? Voice also involves who, in the documentary, is dominant and functions as the spokesperson.

Graphics. Everyone who is interviewed should be identified, and important elements of the documentary should be described, by keying in a caption at the appropriate time. The caption should be left on screen for a short while, then faded off.

Sound Effects. Capturing natural sound and using sound effects, in particular instances, are important components of documentaries. In scripts, sound effects are written in at the proper places, in the manner described earlier in the sample of a documentary script provided in Chapter 2.

Exercises

1. Prepare a 10-page documentary. This assignment will be a simulation. Material from books and articles will be considered as being the equivalent of actual interviews. A documentary maker would make a number of video and sound recordings of actual interviews with authorities or people involved with

some topic being investigated. For this exercise, quote from articles and books by various people instead of actually recording them. A list of steps to be taken in "making" your documentary follows:

Commit yourself to a subject. Pass in a one-page description of the documentary containing the following elements:

- (a) The subject of the documentary. Do not make any changes later on.
- (b) The projected title of the documentary. The title can be changed if you think of a better one.
- (c) Five different bibliographical sources (articles and books) that you will be using for your quotations. Do not use real interviews because there is no way to determine that these interviews actually took place. Also, experience shows that students often find it extremely difficult to obtain good interviews. It is also a great deal of trouble transposing them from tape to written form. It is much easier to photocopy an article or chapter from a book.

Make a "documentary packet." Make a copy of this packet for your own use later when you actually write the script for your documentary. This packet should consist of the following:

- (a) Six to ten pages of interviews, written in a question-and-answer format. All the dialogue in your documentary should be taken from these pages, so select good material. (You can use only the footage you've shot and the dialogue you've recorded when you really make a documentary.)
- (b) A one-page shot sheet. This is invented by you, and indicates the kinds of shots you think you will be using in making your documentary.

Prepare your 10-page documentary. Double-space all dialogue. This is your final script, which uses only the dialogue recorded in your dialogue sheets, shots (which you invent to suit your purposes), and dialogue by a narrator (which you can add). Remember, the narration should not be dominant. The general rule here is this: Show, don't tell.

2. Record and analyze a documentary. Consider the following questions:

Did the documentary hold your interest?
Did it have any impact on you?
Did you learn anything from it?
What was the purpose of the documentary?

What techniques did the documentary maker use?
Was the documentary fair or did it distort things?
How would you rate the documentary, technically speaking?
Did it have good visuals?
Was it edited well?
Was the sound good?
If you were making the documentary, what would you have
    done differently?

News as Drama

When he was executive producer for nightly news programming at NBC, Reuven Frank supposedly wrote the following memo:

Every news story should, without any sacrifice of probity or responsibility, display the attributes of fiction, or drama. It should have structure and conflict, problem and denouement, rising action and falling action, a beginning, a middle, and an end. These are not only the essentials of drama; they are the essentials of narrative.

—quoted in E. J. Epstein, *News from Nowhere* (1974, pp. 4-5)

9

News

Television stations make a great deal of income from their local news broadcasts (which is one reason that national news broadcasts are limited to 30 minutes), and studies show that most people get their news from television, and give it higher ratings, as far as credibility is concerned, than they give news in print. This is because people watching television are able to see, with their own eyes, footage of events. What they seldom consider is that what they see is what whoever is controlling the camera wants them to see, and that the stories they are offered are those some news director thinks they should know about, will want to know about, or will find intriguing and entertaining.

What Is News?

Generally speaking, news is about events, about what's going on, especially when these events have social and political significance or a public impact. The term *news* applies to written stories, radio accounts, or television "packages" journalists make about these events. If one wanted to be somewhat cynical, one could define *news* as whatever editors think it is.

Traditionally, when we think about news, we want to know answers to the following questions:

- WHAT happened?
- WHO is involved?
- WHERE did it take place?
- WHEN did it happen?
- WHY did it happen?
- HOW will it affect us?

In print journalism, these questions are usually discussed in the first paragraph of a story, so a reader can get the big picture immediately. As the story progresses, other details are added. Different newspapers have different styles of writing stories. In the *New York Times*, for example, stories are often quite long and detailed, while *USA Today* has very short stories and, some suggest, tries to simulate television news.

In commercial television news, the stories are very short as a rule, which is why television news is sometimes described as a "headline service." Stories without visuals that are read by anchors usually last 20 to 30 seconds; voice-overs, stories that are read and that have one visual, usually last 30 to 60 seconds; and packages, stories made by reporters, last 1 to 2 minutes. Of course, viewers get to see events and the people involved in them, so the pictorial element conveys a good deal of information. Radio news must be more descriptive; it can carry interviews, but it also uses very short reports.

Although news stories are supposed to be "reports" that are factual and impartial, these stories can be made dramatic—by emphasizing conflict or focusing on personalities, for example. When we dramatize news, however, we "charge" it with emotion and change it.

There is also the matter of "interpretive reporting." Reporters may stick to the facts, but which facts do they select as the ones worth telling? The element of selectivity is always a problem, even when a reporter is trying to be as objective as possible. In some cases, critics suggest, reporters and editors are trying to be truthful and objective, but, without realizing it, are biased. This is reflected in the stories they select and the ways these stories are put together.

One other matter we must keep in mind involves attribution, which is the use of sources to give a story credibility or to suggest that one has doubts about some aspect of a story (such as information from an anonymous source). In broadcast news, attribution usually goes at the beginning of a story, so listeners know something about the source as they hear the story.

Whether or not attribution is to be used is a matter of professional judgment, except in crime stories, where attribution is always used. Attribution, in such stories, shows that reliable sources are being utilized. In some cases, because of time limitations, it is necessary to forgo naming actual agencies and use instead phrases such as *official sources* or *government sources.*

Categories of News

There are three *kinds* of news: local, national, and international. In television, stations tend to feature local news, leaving national and international news to the network news broadcasts. (Since there are about 6 minutes of commercials on the typical network news show, this means there are only 24 minutes available for reportage on national and international events.) In addition, local news is often sensationalistic—about robberies, murders, rapes, fires, and that kind of thing. The time devoted to news stories in local news shows is also limited, since these broadcasts also deal with sports and the weather. In the late afternoons, some local news broadcasts are much longer, so they have more time for reporting on national and international news, but even here this coverage tends to be quite limited.

There are two categories of news as far as the approach to the subject is concerned: hard news and soft news. Hard news involves "breaking" stories (ones involving immediate events) or important social, political, and economic matters and is about controversial issues. It deals with such things as bills being considered in Congress, decisions of the Supreme Court, reports on the economy by various agencies and organizations, presidential initiatives involving international trade and arms control treaties, and information about pressing social problems such as the AIDS epidemic and the homeless.

Soft news covers everything else: sports, features, "human interest" stories, profiles, entertainment, weather reports, segments on taste and food, and so on. It appeals to our curiosity about celebrities and our interest in local sports teams and deals with things that are usually trivial. (A glance at newspapers will show that they, too, are made up, in large part, of soft news.)

One of the problems editors face is in satisfying the insatiable hunger audiences seem to have for soft news and having time for the really important hard news. All editors must decide whether they should give people what they want or what they need (in terms of the editors' definition of need, that is). One reason this is an important matter is that since people now get much (or most) of their news from television and radio, this has an impact upon their political decision making.

Some media theorists argue that news has the function of *agenda-setting*; people can't make decisions about things they don't know about, so the news they get, this theory suggests, ultimately shapes the way they vote and think about politics and society. So television news is very important.

Television Newswriting

News should be written in a style that is conversational, informal, and simple. Since the ear cannot easily follow long, complex sentences, you must use short sentences, generally of no more than 10 to 15 words. Television news is also very formulaic: It is almost always made up of stories that are read, voice-overs, and packages. Examine the sample television news script in Exhibit 9.1 in terms of the style of writing and the format.

There are a number of terms used in writing scripts for television news broadcasts that one must know, as the television news script shows. Some of the most important follow:

Slugs. These are words that are used to identify a news story. If a story develops, composite slugs can be used, to link new developments to the original story. The slug goes at the top of the page, with the reporter's name and the date of the broadcast.

Actualities. This refers to field recordings, made via audiotape or videotape (or both) of events or interviews. The term is used primarily in radio news.

Bites. These are portions of an interview that are used in a news program.

Sound bites. These are portions of a videotaped interview that are used in news programs.

Exhibit 9.1: Television News Script

Slugline Instructions for Director	Aircrash/AAB/11PM
O/C or LIVE	A DC-10 crashed into an Iowan cornfield today at 2:00 P.M. but nobody was killed. Two engines failed and the pilot had to make an emergency landing in a field just outside of Des Moines.
VO BEGINS	(VO) The plane is all banged up . . . but the corn cushioned the plane and . . . miraculously nobody was killed and only a dozen people were injured, none seriously.
O/C	And now a report from Jim Smith, who is on the scene.
LIVE REMOTE	This is Jim Smith. I have one of the passengers . . . Mary Smith . . . who was on the plane. What was it like when you found out the plane needed to make an emergency landing?
FULL CG MARY SMITH	(CG) We were all scared . . . especially as the plane seemed to be out of control. But there wasn't a panic or anything like that.
O/C	Thanks for that report Jim. And now we have the director of the National Air Safety Commission giving a briefing to the press.

Packages. These are stories that are videotaped in the field that are put together with a reporter's narration. A package then is made of sound bites and reportorial narration. Packages are generally short, and last anywhere from less than a minute to several minutes. The package is the basic element in television news.

Standups. This refers to a videotaped (generally) segment of a package made by a reporter on location somewhere—in the field.

Leads. Leads are the way we start stories and are meant to catch the attention of members of the audience and give them a sense of what the story is about. Leads are the equivalent of a headline and first sentence of a newspaper story and must be carefully written to arouse curiosity and keep the members of the audience tuned in. They also must be short, usually from 6 to 10 words.

Bridges. These are extremely brief transitions between one element in a story and something else. Bridges establish continuity.

Tracks. These are portions of narrated field reports that are usually written out and recorded in the newsroom. Tracks are often used as bridges.

Closer. This refers to the way a reporter ends a package. The closer must satisfy the members of the audience and wrap up the package in a convincing way.

Television news, because it is so technologically complex, has a whole language of its own, but all news stories, whatever the medium, have a number of the elements listed above—in particular, leads, bridges, quotations (the print equivalent of sound bites), and closers. They are basic to the logical structure of news stories.

The Television News Script Format

Television news scripts use the standard split-page format discussed earlier, with video instructions on the left and the news copy (often called the copy block) on the right. Different stations vary the way they want scripts prepared, but Exhibit 9.1 shows a typical format. There are a number of terms used to guide newscasters that must be learned. The most important of these terms, which appear in the video column, are as follows:

(1) *O/C* (on camera) or *live*. This means the copy is being read from the studio.

(2) *VO* (voice-over). In this case, the announcer is off camera and reads copy "over" the visual material that is shown on the screen.

(3) *Full CG* (character generator). Here a caption is going to be used on the screen. Usually the material to be used in the caption is written in also.

(4) *SOT* (sound on tape). Here both sound and video come from the videotape.

(5) *Remote*. This term is used for something broadcast directly from the field. *Live remote* refers to a live broadcast, shot from someplace out of the studio, usually where something of importance is taking place.

(6) *TRT* (total running time). This term is used specifically for the amount of time a tape runs.

Radio News Script Format

Radio news scripts are relatively simple in design. This is because radio is a much less complicated medium than television, using only an announcer's voice and, in some instances, recordings of interviews or actualities. There are a few important terms to know, however:

(1) *Carts*. These are cartridges with actualities or interviews that are used, in appropriate places, in the radio news broadcast.

(2) *Incues* (ICs). Incues usually contain the first four or five words of the interview, which allows people to make sure they are using the correct cart and that it is cued in the proper manner.

(3) *Outcues*. These contain the last four or five words of the cart and help directors or engineers cue newscasters, so they can resume reading the news script. Outcues are needed to prevent gaps or dead air in the newscasts.

Exhibit 9.2 provides an example of a radio script format, using the same story reported in Exhibit 9.1 for television. Note that in radio news scripts, technical information is circled, indicating that it is not to be read.

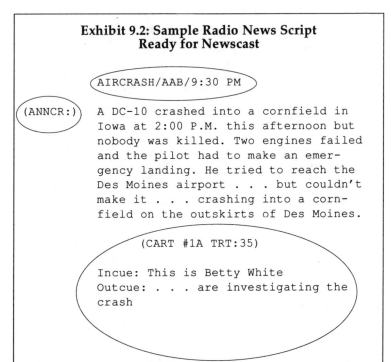

**Exhibit 9.2: Sample Radio News Script
Ready for Newscast**

AIRCRASH/AAB/9:30 PM

(ANNCR:)   A DC-10 crashed into a cornfield in
            Iowa at 2:00 P.M. this afternoon but
            nobody was killed. Two engines failed
            and the pilot had to make an emer-
            gency landing. He tried to reach the
            Des Moines airport . . . but couldn't
            make it . . . . crashing into a corn-
            field on the outskirts of Des Moines.

            (CART #1A TRT:35)

            Incue: This is Betty White
            Outcue: . . . are investigating the
            crash

There are variations in the way radio scripts are formatted,
and the way terms are used, but, generally speaking, radio
scripts have the following elements.

(1) *A slug for the story, the initials of the reporter, and the time and date
    the story is to be broadcast* on the top line of the page.

(2) *One-inch margins on each side of the page.* Generally, one-inch
    margins used on both sides of a page give a line (using pica type)
    that takes about .04 minutes to read, so a 45-second story would
    take 12 lines. (In the print world, newspaper stories are assigned
    in terms of inches, with four lines of typewritten material adding
    up to an inch of printed text.)

(3) *Double-spaced copy, using caps and lowercase.* Some newsrooms
    prefer all caps, but we will use caps and lowercase, because it is
    easier to read material written that way.

(4) *Information about the carts.* This includes the cartridge number, information on the tape running time (TRT), the length of the material to be used, and both the incue and the outcue.

(5) *The word* Announcer *(ANNCR) preceding material to be read.*

(6) *Circles around any material that isn't to be read.* This prevents the announcer or whoever is reading the copy from getting confused.

Helpful Hints for Writing News Copy

In writing news copy there are a number of conventions that are generally followed. Some of the more important of these are listed below:

(1) *Do not use internal punctuation.* Commas are indicated by three dots (ellipses), apostrophes are used for contractions and possessives, and periods and question marks are used at the ends of sentences.

(2) *Spell out numbers from one to eleven and use numerals for all others.* You can, however, use numbers for dates. Spell out all numbers above 999 (for example: one, two, eleven, 12, 999, one-thousand and ten).

(3) *Don't use acronyms, except for institutions everyone knows.* It is okay to use F-B-I (spelled out, with hyphens between letters, indicating you sound out the letters) or NATO or UNESCO (in which you sound out the word), but aside from ones that are commonly known, write out in full the names of all organizations and institutions.

(4) *Write out all symbols.* To make sure your reader doesn't get confused by symbols, write them out.

(5) *Avoid causing sibilance.* A series of words that begin with or contain the letter S sometimes causes a hissing sound and should be avoided.

(6) *Write in the active voice.* As I discussed in Chapter 2, when writing for the ear, especially, the active voice is much livelier than the passive ("John loves ice cream" as opposed to "Ice cream is loved by John").

(7) *Always read your scripts out loud after you have written them.* Frequently your ear picks up things and recognizes problems that have escaped your eye.

This chapter on writing broadcast news is intended to introduce a subject that is extremely complicated. At many institutions, newswriting is the subject of a semester-long course, and
there are a number of books on writing broadcast news, such as
John Hewitt's excellent text, *Air Words: Writing for Broadcast
News,* which I have drawn upon in writing this chapter.

Though this chapter has been somewhat schematic, it does
offer readers a broad overview of the subject, and, together with
the examples offered and material to be added by instructors,
should provide a good introduction to broadcast newswriting.

Exercises

1. Take a news article from the front page of your local paper
and rewrite it as a 50-word radio news item and as a 50-word
(words of dialogue) television news item. You can invent any
shots you want or anything else you will need to write the story.
Remember to keep your lead short—from 6 to 10 words.

2. This is a class project. Use VCRs to tape the national news
broadcasts from the three networks for the same time period of
the same day and compare them. Also record the *MacNeil/Lehrer
NewsHour* for that day and purchase a copy of the *New York
Times* and your local newspaper for that same day. List all of the
network news stories, and record how long they lasted. Note
any differences between the information provided in stories
about the same subject as well as differences in the points of
view. List the stories on *MacNeil/Lehrer* and how long they
lasted.

Answer the following questions:

(a) In what ways were the network news programs similar and in
     what ways were they different? Did they cover the same stories?
     If so, how do you explain that? If not, how do you explain that?
(b) What "general picture" of things emerged from each of the
     network shows? Did you detect any bias in the stories?
(c) How did the network news "lists" (in the industry, the term
     used is *stack*) of stories differ from the *MacNeil/Lehrer* list? How
     did the news shows differ (aside from the fact that *MacNeil/
     Lehrer* lasts an hour)? What about the selection of the stories?
     Did you find bias there?

(d) If you were made a network news director and given an hour for your newscast, what differences would you make in the broadcast?

(e) How do the various news broadcasts differ from the picture of things presented by the *New York Times* and your local newspaper?

3. Design a comedy news show. You must add some genre (game show, science fiction, soap opera, or whatever) to the news genre. Write a three-page television script for this show. You can make up the news stories you wish to use, and can employ any of the 45 humor techniques you want in doing this. Keep "good taste" and propriety in mind when you do this exercise.

4. This is another comedy writing exercise. Find a "soft" news story about some movie star or celebrity and write 50-word accounts of it as they might be broadcast on radio news shows from any three of the following countries: the Soviet Union, Japan, England, France, Italy, Germany, Iran, Cuba, Brazil, Australia. Be sure to use the appropriate accents and to satirize various aspects of the culture and society being dealt with. Make certain you do not insult any racial or ethnic group, or members of either sex or persons of any sexual orientation, when doing this exercise.

Note: When you write straight news stories, avoid trying to include comedy in them. It seldom works. If there is something funny about your story, the story itself should generate the humor (without your "help"). This is an exercise in writing comedy that satirizes news, *not* a newswriting exercise.

I like the slow, smooth roll of the great big trains—and they are the best trains in the world! I like being drawn through the green country and looking at it through the clear glass of the great windows. Though, of course, the country isn't really green. The sun shines, the earth is blood red, and purple and red, and green and red. And the oxen in the ploughlands are bright varnished brown and black and blackish purple; and the peasants are dressed in the black and white of magpies; and there are great flocks of magpies, too. Or the peasants' dresses in another field where there are little mounds of hay that will be grey-green on the sunny side and purple in the shadows—the peasants' dresses are vermilion with emerald green ribbons and purple skirts and white shirts and black velvet stomachers. Still, the impression is that you are drawn through brilliant green meadows that run away on each side to the dark purple fir-woods; the basalt pinnacles; the immense forests.

—Ford Maddox Ford, *The Good Soldier:*
A Tale of Passion (1960, pp. 41-42)

10

Public Service Announcements

Public service announcements (PSAs) are one of the simplest and most mechanical genres found on radio and television. But they pose some problems for writers, because of the need to convey information in an easily understandable manner in relatively limited time periods.

PSAs have the following characteristics:

(1) *They are usually read by announcers or disk jockeys.* You do not usually find dialogue or production values in PSAs, though some nationally produced ones do have dramatic elements in them.

(2) *They are free.* This is because PSAs are broadcast for organizations or agencies that are nonprofit and function in the public's behalf. Thus the announcements are broadcast as a "public service" by radio and television stations. Radio and television stations use airwaves "owned" by the public and thus offer PSAs in partial payment, so to speak, for this privilege.

(3) *They are generally provided on a sheet with announcements of varying lengths.* Often, you find PSAs written to take 10 seconds, 20 seconds, 30 seconds, or 60 seconds (see Exhibit 10.1).

(4) *They are simple and straightforward.* It is difficult to inject much personality and style into a PSA, but that doesn't mean it can't be done, and, in certain situations, PSAs can be entertaining. But the main thrust of the PSA is to convey information clearly and succinctly. In writing a PSA, you must be careful to avoid long sentences. Also, don't offer too much information. The main thing is to keep things simple.

(5) *They include a contact person (or persons) with telephone numbers and release date on the sheet carrying the PSAs.* This is done so stations have someone to contact in case there are questions

133

Exhibit 10.1: Sample PSAs

10-Second Public Service Announcement

```
"Incredible Insects" . . . All you ever wanted
to know about insects . . . July 2 through Sep-
tember 7 . . . at Coyote Point Museum . . .
Call 342-7755.
```

20-Second Public Service Announcement

```
Insects can be found in the air . . . in water
. . . and on land. They can also be found at
Coyote Point Museum in the exhibit . . .
"Incredible Insects" . . . July 2 through
September 7 . . . call 342-7755.
```

30-Second Public Service Announcement

```
Insects can be found in the air . . . in water
. . . and on land. They can also be found on
exhibit at Coyote Point Museum in San Mateo
. . . July 2 through September 7 . . . the
exhibit . . . "Incredible Insects" . . . uses
large models . . . specimens . . . photos and
text . . . to open our eyes to the insect world
. . . Call 342-7755.
```

Used by permission of the Coyote Point Museum.

about the PSA. Sheets carrying PSAs generally carry a "For Immediate Release" tag and often a "stop date" tag.

Exercise

1. Find a notice in print about some meeting or event that a nonprofit or service organization is having and write 10-second, 20-second, 30-second, and 60-second PSAs for that

meeting or event. Attach the print notice to a second sheet of paper. If you obtain information about some service offered by a nonprofit organization, you can write PSAs about that service. Be sure that you are writing a PSA for an organization or entity that is nonprofit and therefore entitled to use PSAs.

A statement is persuasive and credible either because it is directly self-evident or because it appears to be proved from other statements that are so. In either case, it is persuasive because there is somebody whom it persuades. . . . The duty of rhetoric is to deal with such matters as we deliberate upon without arts or systems to guide us, in the hearing of persons who cannot take in at a glance a complicated argument, to follow a long chain of reasoning. The subjects of our deliberation are such as seem to present us with alternative possibilities: about things that could have been, and cannot now or in the future be, other than they are, nobody who takes them to be of this nature wastes his time in deliberation.

—Aristotle, *Rhetoric*, Book I, Chapter 2

11

Editorials

An editorial is a statement of "station" opinion, usually representing views of the owner or manager of a radio or television station (or the station's "editorial committee"), that deals with some issue of social and political significance. Private individuals also have access to radio and television stations, usually to offer rebuttals to editorials that has been broadcast by the station. Some stations also offer individuals time for "free speech" or public opinion messages.

The following are suggestions for writing good editorials.

The topic of the editorial should be worth considering. It should be on some issue of public importance about which there are varying views and that has important implications or consequences. The editorial should not be wasted on trivial matters, and should not be what amounts to a public service announcement praising an organization.

The writer of the editorial should use the editorial "we". This shows that the view is not offered as a purely personal one but as representative of, for example, the station.

Although editorials are statements of opinion, they must be based on "facts" and "data." That is, the editorial must offer the viewer or listener some kind of evidence (statistics, data, information, reports by reputable agencies) that supports the position taken by the editorial. It is not enough to say "we believe" without offering reasons for having a particular position. In the case of television editorials, you can use footage when relevant and give part of the editorial as a voice-over. For example, if you are offering an editorial supporting an organization that helps the homeless, you can give part of the editorial as a voice-over while you show footage of the organization at work, so people can see for themselves what the organization is doing and get some idea of how effective it is.

The argument made in the editorial must be a logical one. You must be careful not to make logical errors or to use incorrect ways of arguing in your editorial. Argument styles to avoid include the following:

- using emotionally toned words
- offering selected instances as proof
- misrepresenting views of opponents
- appealing to authority
- trying to convince by using a confident tone (bluffing)
- oversimplifying and saying an "either/or" situation exists
- using false authorities (not experts on subject in question)
- moving from *some* to *all* (overgeneralizing)
- making false assumptions ("everyone knows")

Mention one or two arguments made by those with opposing views, and refute them as best you can. What makes editorials difficult is that they are frequently about issues that are complicated and on which all kinds of people have different views. In your arguments for or against a particular course of action, you should offer evidence that reasonable people would accept as valid, and focus on two or three arguments to avoid confusing listeners.

Write in an interesting, coherent, and confident manner. Try to give your editorial something that will help people remember it. You must be clear about what the topic of the editorial is and what your position on the issue under discussion is.

Come to some conclusion. When relevant, end with a call to action of some kind (such as "Write a letter of support to us and we will send it on to your representatives in Congress," or "Write to Congressman Smith and Senator Jones and let them know that you want them to vote for this bill.").

Exhibits 11.1 and 11.2 provide examples of two editorials, one used on radio, the other on television.

Exhibit 11.1: Example of a Radio Editorial

WELCOME TO THE WORKING WEEK

(HERE IS KCBS GENERAL MANAGER RAY BARNETT WITH
AN EDITORIAL OPINION.)

What's the reward for hard work? Poverty . . .
for millions of Americans who work at the minimum wage. A full-time job at the minimum wage
pays less than seven thousand dollars a year
. . . well under the poverty line for a family
of three.

KCBS thinks that's a disgrace. For the last six
years, the minimum wage has been stuck at 3.35
an hour. While the price of almost everything
goes higher and higher . . . for many Americans,
the fruits of their labors are becoming smaller
and smaller.

Who are these people? Most of them . . . 4 out
of 5 in California . . . are adults. More than
25 percent of workers at the minimum wage are
heads of households. There are teenagers and
part-timers working for the minimum . . . but
for many people, the minimum wage isn't a dues-
paying job, or a little money in the side . . .
it's their job . . . period.

California's Industrial Welfare Commission will
meet after this summer to consider an increase
in the state minimum wage. The state Assembly
and Senate have passed legislation to raise
California's minimum to 4.25 an hour next year.
And Congress is working on a proposal to increase the federal minimum wage to 4.65 an hour
by 1990.
KCBS believes no one working a full-time job
should be paid a part-time wage. We think an increase in the minimum wage is long overdue. But
there's strong opposition to any increase . . .
so your voice needs to be heard. We'll tell YOU
how to get involved. Call us at 765-4124.

BROADCAST: July 6, 1987; 5:22a, 9:25a, 12:42p,
6:26p.

Exhibit 11.2: Example of a Television Editorial

```
                              EDITORIAL #34
Telecast: January 20, 1988 - Sign On, Noon News,
                              6PM News, Overnight
                              News
          January 22, 1988 - 11PM News
          January 23, 1988 - Sign On, 6:30PM
                              News, After CBS Sun-
                              day Night News,
                              Overnight News
          January 25, 1988 - People Are Talking
By Carolyn Wean, Vice President and General
Manager
```

ACT FOR BETTER CHILDCARE (SB 1885)

In a recent KPIX survey we learned that
childcare is a critical issue for most parents
with young children. That's why we support both
local and national efforts to make childcare a
political priority in 1988.

It's a fact that 63% of mothers with children
under 18 are in the labor force. Over half of
mothers with children under one year are working. And we know too that on the average, a working parent will miss one week of work each year
because of childcare problems.

Whether we like it or not, traditional roles
have changed. Mothers who used to stay home and
care for young children now have to work; the
two paycheck family is here to stay.
Both Democrats *and* Republicans are accepting
this as a fact of life. Senate Bill 1885 is a bi-
partisan plan to help working parents. Over 100
national organizations support it. What it will
do is this: Two and a half billion dollars will
be allocated to the fifty states to make
childcare available to parents *and* to train
childcare workers. California will be eligible
for $225 million a year for five years. Low in-
come parents will have the first priority, but
middle income families will also be eligible. If

(continued)

Exhibit 11.2 Continued

the bill passes, parents who work will then have peace of mind that their children are safe and in centers that meet federal health and safety requirements. And this will ultimately benefit all of us. This plan is called the A-B-C Bill—Act For Better Childcare. It's the most important bill of its kind ever to be drafted.

It's in committee now, and it needs our support. Write to Senators Cranston and Wilson and to your congressmen. Tell them the time has come to get realistic about childcare in America.

For Kids' Sake and for our sake, let's get this bill passed.

I'm Carolyn Wean.

Used by permission of KPIX.

Exercises

1. Tape some editorials given on your local television and radio stations. Analyze these editorials in terms of the considerations mentioned above, with a particular concern for the use of logic and methods of persuasion employed in the editorials.

2. Select editorials from a newspaper and analyze them the way you've analyzed the broadcast editorials.

3. Take a subject of local social and political significance and find some substantive articles about it in a local newspaper. Use these articles as your source of information for writing a radio editorial of 125 words (approximately one minute). Make sure you don't use any incorrect means of arguing.

WHY DON'T YOU—YES BUT

Thesis. "Why Don't You—Yes But" occupies a special place in game analysis, because it was the original stimulus for the concept of games. It was the first game to be dissected out of its social context, and since it is the oldest subject of game analysis, it is one of the best understood. It is also the game most commonly played at parties and groups of all kinds, including psychotherapy groups. The following example will serve to illustrate its main characteristics.

White: "My husband always insists on doing our own repairs, and he never builds anything right."

Black: "Why doesn't he take a course in carpentry?"

White: "Yes, but he doesn't have time."

Black: "Why don't you buy him some good tools?"

White: "Yes, but he doesn't know how to use them."

Red: "Why don't you have your building done by a carpenter?"

White: "Yes, but that would cost too much."

Brown: "Why don't you just accept what he does the way he does it?"

White: "Yes, but the whole thing might fall down."

Such an exchange is typically followed by a silence. It is eventually broken by Green, who may say something like, "That's men for you, always trying to show how efficient they are."

—Eric Berne, *Games People Play* (1964)

12

Reviews

Reviews are similar to editorials in that they are statements of opinion, but they are made by a particular reviewer and they are about works of art, typically films, plays, and television shows. In this chapter we will deal with film reviews, but it isn't very difficult to apply the same criteria used in evaluating films to plays or television shows.

The following are aspects of film reviews:

Film reviews are a form of entertainment. As such, they should be lively and interesting. The review should have vitality and personality. As a reviewer, you will be judged on both the strength and the correctness of your evaluations of films and the quality of your presentations. If you pan a film but the audience at the screening loved it, you might want to mention that.

Reviews offer listeners a sense of what the film is about. In some cases, there is considerable detail about the plot, in others, just a broad summary. But listeners want to know something about the plot of a film that is being reviewed. Sound bites of important lines of dialogue can be used in a review. This helps listeners get a sense of what the film is like.

When you write a review, you might want to say something about the genre of the film. Is it a light comedy, a spy thriller, an action-adventure film, a science fiction film, or some combination of genres? Is this film like any other film (in ways that you can discuss) with which the listener might be familiar? You might comment on the quality of the script. Was the dialogue good? If you are reviewing a comedy, was the dialogue amusing, witty, clever, and entertaining? Were there any memorable lines (to use in a sound bite)?

Reviews are often placed within the context of competing films or of trends. They give some kind of background for the listener. There is also information about how the film was made, where it was made, and problems that were encountered in making it. In some cases, the film might have a social, political, or ideological dimension to it. Some films deal specifically with social problems, historical incidents, or social issues (racism, anti-Semitism, sexism, greed).

Reviews discuss the quality of the acting. Who is in the film? Are there any big stars in it? What other films have they made? How good are they? Are there any extraordinary performances? Arc there any really poor performances? Who gave them? Why were performers lacking? Were actors miscast?

Reviews often report on the style of the director. Who directed the film? What were some of his or her previous films with which listeners may be familiar? Is there anything distinctive about his or her style of directing? How does this film rate when compared with previous films made by the director? Are there technical aspects of interest?

Reviews come to some kind of a conclusion about the film and offer listeners a personal opinion. Is this film a "must see" or a real "dog" or, perhaps, something that only certain kinds of people might like? Reviews discuss how the film is doing at the box office, for example, and how it has been received, in general, by other critics. It has been said that "there's no accounting for taste," and that probably is true. But in offering a review of a film, the reviewer offers listeners reasons for any conclusions. A review, then, like a lawyer's argument, is based upon "evidence" (upon evaluations of the various aspects of the film); but, unlike the case in law, the reviewer is lawyer, judge, jury, and, in some cases, chief executioner. A reviewer must make certain, of course, that all statements of fact are correct, because if listeners discover that facts are wrong, they won't give much credence to the review.

A film review (or any review) depends upon the taste, the expertise, the background, and the style of the reviewer. Film reviews are a form of journalism (and some would say a form of advertising as well) and must be entertaining.

The more you know, obviously, the more you see. Some film reviews, written in magazines such as the *New Yorker*, run on for many pages and often go into great (in some cases excruciating) detail. On the other hand, radio film reviews don't have the luxury of thousands of words. A radio film review must be brief, to the point, and written in a relatively simple style. But it can still do wonders, even with these limitations. Exhibit 12.1 presents an example of a radio film review; it is reproduced here by permission of radio station KNBR-AM, San Francisco.

Exhibit 12.1: Sample Radio Movie Review

JAN WAHL, *movie critic and talk-show host, KNBR-AM, San Francisco*

Broadcast August 14, 1989, 8:35 a.m., on the *Frank & Mike Show*

It's Monday, so we do new videos. A little controversy now. The name of the movie is *The Last Temptation of Christ*. It's now out on video. This is based on the novel by Nikos Kazantzakis. He got into a lot of trouble for writing this thing. Martin Scorsese got into loads of trouble for directing it. You remember, of course, the great controversy. It's a story of Jesus but showing him as a man, with all of a man's confusions and torments. Also humor . . . There's humor in this film because, after all, life is about humor. And this is just a human being who finds himself in the strange position of being the son of God. You know, things are tough all over. Martin Scorsese has created a world filled with people we can relate to. I mean, yes, so the apostles have kind of Brooklyn accents, you know. But what makes it interesting is they suddenly become people rather than biblical symbols, and this is very important. Willem Dafoe is brilliant as Jesus. You see everything going on internally. I voted for Martin Scorsese to get the DGA award, the Directors Guild Award, last year. That's how powerful the scenes are. Each of these scenes stands on its own. There's one scene in the desert that will be etched in your mind forever, as one you'll never forget, as Jesus tries to find out what God has in mind for him. What this film does is it takes the story and makes you ask questions about it. And that's one of the best things a movie can do is make you look inside yourself. So I highly recommend *The Last Temptation of Christ*. I say start it early in the evening. It's not for kids, but start it early. It makes you think, it makes you almost feel like you've had a religious experience.

Exercises

1. Find reviews of a particular film in a number of different publications, such as your local newspaper, the *New York Times*, the *New Yorker, Jump Cut,* and various film journals. Compare them. What did you learn from looking at the different kinds of reviews and perspectives on reviewing?

2. Write a 300- to 350-word radio review of a film that has just been released. Compare your review with the reviews of professionals on radio and in the print media. Did you neglect anything of consequence in your review? Did you disagree with other critics about matters such as the acting, directing, or technical aspects of the film?

3. Some philosophers argue that "beauty is in the eye of the beholder." Do you believe that there is no such thing as an intrinsically "beautiful" painting or beautiful woman (which would be the case if that statement were true)? Do you think there are objective standards for what makes a film good or bad, or is everything, ultimately, a matter of opinion? If there is "no accounting for taste," does that mean that nobody's taste is better than anyone else's taste or does it mean, instead, that it is hard to explain why one person's taste is better than another's?

"Your Majesty [said Holmes], as I understand, became entangled with this young person, wrote her some compromising letters, and is now desirous of getting those letters back."

"Precisely so. But how—"

"Was there a secret marriage?"

"None."

"No legal papers or certificates?"

"None."

"Then I fail to follow your Majesty. If this young person should produce letters for blackmailing or other purposes, how is she to prove their authenticity?"

"There is the writing."

"Pooh, pooh! Forgery."

"My private notepaper."

"Stolen."

"My own seal."

"Imitated."

"My photograph."

"Bought."

"We were both in the photograph."

"Oh dear! That is very bad! Your Majesty has indeed created an indiscretion."

— A. Conan Doyle, "A Scandal in Bohemia,"
from *The Adventures of Sherlock Holmes*

13

Teleplays

Teleplay is the term that is often used for a play that is written for television. The important part of the term here is *play*, for it is the quality of the writing that is crucial. Great plays written for the stage televise well, because they are beautifully written. In television as in theater, "the play's the thing."

Formulas in Television

These plays can vary from situation comedies to action-adventure shows. Most of the genres or kind of plays carried on television tend to be highly formulaic, with rather conventional plots and familiar kinds of characters. These formulas are important, because writers don't have a great deal of time (especially in 22-minute teleplays) to develop character and create complicated plots. As people watch television, they get used to seeing certain kinds of characters, situations, and settings, and to hearing certain kinds or styles of dialogue; the writers of teleplays can take this for granted and use it to get things going quickly.

Thus formulas are useful because they provide writers and audiences with common grounds of understanding. This does not mean that formulas cannot be violated, or used in creative ways. It merely means that when you are writing for gigantic audiences, you have to remember what your audiences are like (and what they like) and you can't get too arty—unless you are looking for a small "niche" audience.

Formulas are also useful because they enable teleplay writers to write more quickly, since they aren't starting from zero with their characters or plots. Television has a voracious need for "product" (plays), which is why teleplay writers find formulas so useful.

The chart that follows, taken from my *Signs In Contemporary Culture: An Introduction to Semiotics*, describes some of the basic genres and their various formulaic elements. This chart, which deals with Westerns (no longer often seen on television, except in old films), science fiction, hard-boiled detective shows (such as *Mickey Spillane's Mike Hammer*), and family sitcoms. But it could easily be extended to other genres, such as soap operas, game shows, and spy shows. It has been suggested by some critics that all popular art genres are formulaic, and that the difference between "elite" art and popular art stems in great part from one being "inventive" and the other being "formulaic." This strikes me as a great oversimplification.

Formulaic Elements in Public Art Forms

Art Form/Genre	Classic Western	Science Fiction	Hard-Boiled Detective	Family Sitcom
Time	1800s	future	present	anytime
Location	edge of civilization	space	city	suburbs
Protagonist	cowboy (lone individual)	astronaut	detective	father (figure)
Heroine	schoolmarm	spacegal	damsel in distress	mother (figure)
Villain	outlaws, killers	aliens	killer	boss, neighbor
Secondary characters	townsfolk, Indians	technicians in spacecraft	cops, underworld	kids, dogs
Plot	restore law and order	repel aliens	find killer	solve problem
Theme	justice	triumph of humanity	pursuit and discovery	chaos and confusion
Costume	cowboy hat, boots, etc.	high-tech uniforms	trench coat	regular clothes
Locomotion	horse	spaceship	beat-up car	station wagon
Weaponry	six-guns, rifles	ray guns	pistols, fists	insults

Whatever the case, anyone who wishes to write for television should learn to look at the various genres carefully and to notice how individual shows use and adapt various formulaic conventions for their own purposes—sometimes very creatively. This analysis should extend to specific episodes of shows, also.

Script Format of Teleplays

Teleplays have a different format from any of the other scripts that have been discussed in this book. In essence, the teleplay format is that of a play, except that room is made for notes about shots. The average teleplay, however, does not go into great detail about the kinds of shots to be used (the way a documentary does, for instance). A sample of a teleplay script is shown in Exhibit 13.1.

Here are some conventions for writing teleplays.

(1) *Dialogue is single-spaced, typed in caps and lowercase, and written in the center of the page, leaving wide margins on either side.* A typical line consists of seven or eight words, at the most. Generally speaking, the dialogue is conversational and the lines characters speak are not very long. After a character's speech is finished, a blank line is left so it is easy to see who is saying what.

(2) *Names of the characters are typed in ALL CAPS in the center of the dialogue.* The dialogue follows directly under the name; do *not* skip a line between the name and the dialogue.

(3) *Directions for scenes, groups of characters, and so on are single spaced and run out to the margins of the page.*

(4) *Directions for specific characters are placed in parentheses and can interrupt dialogue.* These directions tell how a particular line is to be spoken or what the character should be doing.

(5) *Scenes for television are numbered and are written in ALL CAPS and underlined.* A great deal of discretion is left to the director as far as the kinds of shots to be used in a given scene is concerned.

(6) *Shot editing information (CUT, DISSOLVE, FADE OUT) is written in ALL CAPS, underlined, and placed on the right-hand side of the page.* A line is skipped on either side of this information so it stands out.

(7) *Instructions for sound effects (SFX) are written in ALL CAPS and NOT underlined.*

Exhibit 13.1: Sample of a Drama Script Format

Sc. 1 (cont)

Jack looks at Jill strangely, shrugs his shoulders . . .

> NARRATOR
>
> There was something menacing about the hill that Jack and Jill both sensed . . . something dangerous.

> JACK
>
> That hill bothers me . . .

Jill sighs and hands him a pail. He puts it down.

> NARRATOR
>
> Jack didn't know what he was getting into but he couldn't escape that feeling of anxiety as he looked up the hill.

> JILL
>
> Come on Jack, don't be such a scaredy-cat. Let's go. I'm really thirsty . . . and they're expecting us back with some water.

> JACK
> (uncomfortable)
>
> Do we have to, Jill? I'm scared . . . that something bad's gonna happen up there . . . to me . . . and to you.

He starts running away from the path leading to the top of the hill. Jill runs after him, catches him by arm and starts tugging at his arm. He stops and turns, facing her.

> JILL
>
> Let's go. Get your pail . . . I'll come with you, too. There's nothing to worry about.

A BEAT

Exhibit 13.1 Continued

```
(suggestively)
We can have some fun up there on that
hill . . . there's never anyone around up
there, if you know what I mean.
(she winks at Jack and blows him a kiss)

                    JACK
Okay . . . you talked me into it.
```

---

(8) *Teleplays begin with instructions to FADE IN and conclude with instructions to FADE OUT. Act endings are also indicated, in ALL CAPS.*

As a rule of thumb, a 30-minute show (which means around 22 minutes, when you subtract time for promotions and commercials) runs between 25 and 30 pages, or approximately two-thirds of a minute per page of script. During the editing process, final adjustments can be made to get the timing more precise.

The Problem of Story

Everyone will tell you that the most important aspect of television is the writing. If you have an excellent script, all kinds of actors and actresses can be found to give it life. But if you have a poor script, even the best performers can't save it.

When it comes to dramas, you need two basic things: three-dimensional characters with whom the audience can identify, and plots that are interesting and exciting. All writers know this; doing it is what is difficult. Generally speaking, the key to story or plotting is to have some kind of conflict, difficulty, or problem that is tied to the personalities of the characters and that generates the actions that take place.

This conflict can be friendly or unfriendly, it can be essentially intellectual (about ideas) or it can be physical (involving violence)—but one way or another, we must have some kind of conflict, some kind of a problem that must be posed and resolved, through the actions of the main characters (heroes, heroines, villains, and so on). Television is a visual medium and requires a certain amount of action and even spectacle, like theater.

Television writers use particular terms to refer to some of the important elements in teleplays; the list shown in Exhibit 13.2 is drawn from an article by Pamela Eelss et al. titled "Laying Pipe, Add Heat, Get Laughs: The Making of a Television Sitcom," which appeared in *Harper's* (November 1988).

Vladimir Propp to the Rescue

In 1928, Russian folklorist Vladimir Propp made a study of a group of Russian fairy tales and discovered what we might consider to be the "laws of story making." Propp described the basic "functions" found in the stories—using this term to mean "an act of a character defined from the point of view of its significance for the course of the action." We need not go into all the details of Propp's theories here, many of which are not relevant to our concerns.

What is important for our purpose is to recognize that Propp found 30 different functions that are the building blocks of narratives (stories). These actions are found in all stories, from the most ancient Greek plays to contemporary films, and that is because these functions are connected to character and conflict. In using Propp's functions, you must recognize that he was describing fairy tales, so the actions described involve the typical events in fairy tales. But if we do a little bit of imaginative thinking, and modernize the functions and adapt them to contemporary genres, we can see that they really underlie all narratives.

Thus, for example, one of Propp's functions is as follows: "Misfortune is made known, hero is dispatched." This can be applied to the typical James Bond story, in which some British

---

Exhibit 13.2: Screenplay Terminology

Act.
Each half-hour script (which reduces down to 22 minutes, remember) has two 11-minute acts.

Arc.
The way a character develops during an episode of a show.

Backstory.
This refers to the basic circumstances of the show—the important events that got it going. We see this in the opening show of a series.

Bible.
This contains information about the various characters, the backstory, the premise of the show. The Bible allows writers to add new episodes without going astray.

Blowup.
This is the climax of a plot. It usually takes place in the next-to-last scene. The last scene involves the resolution of the blowup.

Heat.
This involves some conflict in an episode that is behind a character's actions.

Laying pipe.
This refers to the way a scene is developed to set up "punch lines" in comedies.

Lighting the lantern.
This involves highlighting or emphasizing some special trait of a character.

Opening up.
This involves introducing a new character or new characters into a series, so as to expand the possibilities for new conflicts and relationships.

Spin.
This follows heat and involves its resolution, one way or another.

---

agents are killed (as in *Dr. No*) and M. sends Bond off to find out what has happened. Another function involves the hero receiving a magic agent. In the Bond stories, this can be applied to the new guns and various "magic" gizmos Bond gets from Q. It is possible to take a typical James Bond episode and find many (if not most) of Propp's functions in it, and the same applies to any other stories you can think of, from those about Indiana Jones to those about Luke Skywalker in *Star Wars*. A list of Propp's functions is provided in Exhibit 13.3; this form of his list originally appeared in an earlier work of mine, *Media Analysis Techniques*.

Propp suggested that there are certain main characters found in stories:

Exhibit 13.3. Propp's Functions

Initial situation	Members of family or hero introduced.
Absentation	One of the members of the family absents himself from home
Interdiction	An interdiction is addressed to the hero.
Violation	An interdiction is violated.
Reconnaissance	The villain makes an attempt at reconnaissance.
Delivery	The villain receives information about his victim.
Trickery	The villain attempts to deceive his victim.
Complicity	The victim submits to deception, unwittingly helps his enemy.
Villainy	The villain causes harm or injury to a member of a family.
Lack	One member of a family lacks something or wants something.
Mediation	Misfortune is made known, hero is dispatched.
Counteraction	Seekers agree to decide on counteraction.
Departure	The hero leaves home.
1st function of donor	Hero is tested, receives magical agent or helper.
Hero's reaction	Hero reacts to actions of the future donor.
Receipt of magic agent	Hero acquires the use of a magical agent.
Spatial transference	Hero led to object of search.
Struggle	Hero and villain join in direct combat.
Branding	Hero is branded.
Victory	Villain is defeated.
Liquidation	Initial misfortune or lack is liquidated.
Return	The hero returns.
Pursuit	A chase: the hero is pursued.
Rescue	Rescue of hero from pursuit.
Unrecognized arrival	The hero, unrecognized, arrives home or in another country.
Unfounded claims	A false hero presents unfounded claims.
Difficult task	A difficult task is proposed to the hero.
Solution	The task is resolved.
Recognition	The hero is recognized.
Exposure	The false hero or villain is exposed.
Transfiguration	The hero is given a new appearance.
Punishment	The villain is punished.

Character	Action
the villain	Fights with hero.
the donor	Gives hero magical agent.
the helper	Helps hero solve difficult tasks.
the princess	Sought-for person.
father of princess	Assigns difficult task for hero.
dispatcher	Sends hero off on mission.
hero	Seeks something or fights villain.
false hero	Claims to be hero, but is unmasked.

All of these characters are drawn from fairy tales, of course, but, properly updated, they can be found in contemporary dramas, also.

The lists of Propp's functions and main characters are meant to provide you with a frame of reference you might want to use in analyzing stories by others and in generating stories yourself. Knowing about the various kinds of characters and their functions may stimulate certain things in your unconscious that will help you invent good characters and create exciting or appealing stories. There is no mechanical way to teach people to be creative, but creative people often are analytical and use what they learn from their investigations of the work of others, and magically, in their own work.

Some narrative theorists believe that all creative works are tied, one way or another, to other works that preceded them. This is not to say that writers consciously try to imitate other writers or want to "steal their stuff," but that on an unconscious level, they are influenced by stories they have seen and read. (Of course, sometimes writers consciously do "borrow" or even "steal" from other writers, without acknowledging what they have done. This type of behavior is highly unethical and is foolish as well, since people who plagiarize are generally caught.)

On Characterization

Characters in teleplays reveal themselves to audiences in a number of different ways (which often interact with one another):

(1) *by what they say* (the language they use)

(2) *by how they say it* (the expressiveness they give to the dialogue)

(3) *by how they look* (their faces, body shapes, clothes)

(4) *by where they live and act* (the symbolic significance of the settings)

(5) *by their body language and facial expression* (how they move and look)

(6) *by what they do* (their actions and reactions)

(7) *by the props they use* (eyeglass styles, jewelry)

In novels, writers can tell you how characters feel about certain things or people, but in teleplays, you have to have the characters either say how they feel or show how they feel (or both). So dialogue becomes extremely important. The various means listed above are ways in which a writer can reveal what characters are like and make them three-dimensional.

One mistake beginning writers often make is to have all the characters speak the same way—essentially through the voice of the writer. The characters must be different and must speak in their own ways if they are to be taken as "real" by audiences. And the style must be conversational, as well, if it is to seem realistic. People generally do not speak in complete sentences when they converse; they use all kinds of contractions and such ("Yeah," "Nah," and so on) and frequently interrupt one another.

The Structure of Teleplays

Since most teleplays are broadcast on commercial television, writers must keep in mind that there will be commercial interruptions. This means that unlike in plays for the theater, where the three-act convention structures the action, in television the numerous commercial breaks structure the action. In order to keep the audience, the action must be such that at each break there is something exciting occurring that will be resolved after the commercial break. So narratives on television usually have a number of crises or exciting moments in them that follow upon one another with great rapidity. They are not like plays found in theaters, which usually have one critical moment, when everything is at stake, that is resolved in the last act.

Propp used the term *moves* for crucial events. In a fairy tale and in films and television plays, there are often a number of tasks to do, problems to deal with, and battles to win. The Indiana Jones films are a good case in point. No sooner does Jones escape from one situation (being held prisoner by the Nazis) than he faces another (being pursued by them), and after he escapes from his pursuers, something else immediately comes up. These films are a bit extreme, as far as the pattern of constant problem and resolution is concerned, but they offer a good example of the kind of thing that has to be done to maintain interest.

Getting Started: The Creative Process

How does one start? That's hard to say. Different writers have different ways of operating, but there are a few approaches or tactics that you might want to consider. Writing a screenplay starts with an idea or a subject that interests you or some image that sticks in your head and keeps bothering you. The crucial thing is to rough in a first draft; after that, you can start revising and get things right. That, at least, is the way Woody Allen works. He says that the hardest thing for him is getting the idea, the concept, the situation that will enable him to write a first draft. After that, things are a lot easier.

Let me suggest some common approaches to the basic problem of getting started. Quite likely, you will use some combination of them when you decide to write your teleplay.

Create some fantastic characters and let them loose. Fiction writers often talk about how their characters "take on lives of their own" and frequently turn out quite different from the way the writers envisioned them. With this approach, you start with the characters and see where your unconscious takes you. You must have a pretty good idea of what each of them is like before you start, even though they may end up surprising you. You might have noticed someone at a party or when you were taking a walk or were shopping at the local grocery. Or maybe you read

about someone in the paper or watched a program about someone who struck a responsive chord.

You say to yourself, "What would happen if I took a character
who is very X and put him into a relationship with one who is
very Y and they had to deal with someone who is very Z?"
These characters must be ones whom viewers will find interesting, ones they can get involved with. So in this approach, the
characters lead you to the plot.

*Think of an exciting plot and let it shape the characters you use to
tell the story.* In this approach, you have some kind of a general
idea of what might happen in your story and it, then, leads you
to the characters who will play the major roles in the telling of
the story. It is the plot that gets you started and that requires
certain kinds of people for the plot to work. You might even
start with a simple situation—something you noticed when you
were out shopping or something suggested by a newspaper
story you read.

Here you say to yourself, "Supposing X, Y, and Z happened?
How would this work? What kinds of characters would I need
to make a story about X, Y, and Z believable?"

In his essay "Portrait of the Writer as a Schizophrenic," Neil
Simon argues that there is a schizoid quality to writers. Generally speaking, they go about living the way everyone else does,
but at certain moments something strikes their attention and
the writer in them takes over. They stop what they are doing
and start "observing" with a view toward how what they are
watching might be used in some work. "What's happening?"
the writers ask themselves. He offers an example. A writer is
sitting on a park bench, enjoying a hot dog with sauerkraut,
when a couple passes by:

> A man and an attractive woman are walking slowly in front of him,
> talking in muted but heated words. He loves her but this can't go
> on. What can't go on? Their marriage? Their affair? Their business
> partnership? Their dance team?

The "monster" in him has taken over. "Monster," he writes,
"leave the world alone. It's none of your business." This is true,
except that this monster is what gives writers ideas for stories,
novels, and plays.

In each of these cases, you would probably do some thinking about both the plot and the characters, and a good place to do this thinking would be in your journal. You might write notes about what your characters look like, their backgrounds, their interests, their tastes, their peculiarities, and so on. You need to have some kind of a general notion before you actually start writing, but it need not be too specific. In the writing itself you will discover or work out many of the details. Often, this comes from revising and inserting things in the script once you've got your first draft roughed in.

A journey of a thousand miles begins with a single step, and a screenplay of 25 pages begins with a first word that is written or keyboarded. But just as travelers don't go off on a thousand-mile trip without some preparation, you can't sit down to write without having done some work on what you will write. And if you have done a good job of preparation, and if you have a good story to tell, and if you are in good form, and if you are lucky, you will experience that peculiar thrill, that feeling of exhilaration and satisfaction, that writers experience when they create something they really like.

Exercises

1. Try writing some short scenes in which you practice writing dialogue. You can do this by cutting stories out of the newspaper and writing scenes that you've adapted from the stories.

2. Read a number of plays and teleplays "technically." That is, see how the writers of these works establish character, use dialogue, develop scenes, and structure their plots. Find a variety of different styles of plays and teleplays, also. Study everyone from Shakespeare to Ionesco, Pirandello to Neil Simon, Rod Serling to Paddy Chayefsky.

3. Videotape an episode of a television series you are familiar with and study it carefully. Notice how the characters speak and what the plots are like, and other particulars of the series. Write a screenplay for the series.

4. Try your hand at comedy. Write a five-page parody of some dramatic show that lends itself to being ridiculed, using a

number of different techniques of comedy: exaggeration, word-play, mistakes, facetiousness, and so on.

5. Start a serial teleplay in your class. Someone starts off by writing two pages, creating some characters and putting them into a situation. Then, each class period, a different person is given the script and asked to write two more pages, which are due the next class period. These pages will be read in class. Thus the script progresses as the course progresses, and by the end of the course, the script will be completed, if the class is small enough.

PART III

Postscripts

Ray Bradbury's method for writing short stories has always been predicated on the question "what if?" What if a 10-year-old boy never ages and is forced to move from town to town, seeking a new family every few years? What if a man plays a trick on a dwarf in a maze of mirrors? What if a little girl drowns in a lake but can't stay dead? What if the wind were a malevolent force and wanted to blow you away? What if a murderer became obsessed with the fear that he left a fingerprint on a piece of fruit in the bottom of a bowl? What if . . . "

John Stanley, "More Magic and Mystery
from Bradbury Machine,"
Datebook, San Francisco Sunday Examiner and Chronicle,
July 9, 1989

14

Common Writing Errors

This chapter deals with a number of common errors that people make when they write. If a script is full of spelling errors, punctuation errors, mechanical errors, and grammatical errors, actors and actresses will become confused when they read the script and try to perform it. You must use the correct script formats when you write for radio and television, but you must also write correctly.

If you can learn to avoid making these errors, your writing will be greatly improved. That is because there are a small number of "repeat offenders" that account for most of the mistakes people make when they write.

To/two/to. People often become confused when using these words. Here is the correct way to use them.

> *Too* equals degree. "Too many, too few, too soon, too late."
> *Two* is a number. "I want two scripts. I need two actors."
> *To* is a preposition. "I am going to Paris, then to London."

You're, Your. Correct use of these forms is as follows:

> *Your* involves possession. "I like your dress."
> *You're* is a contraction. It ties together *you* and *are.* "That's right, you're correct."

There/Their/They're. These confuse many people also.

> *There* stands for a place. "I'm going there in June."
> *Their* involves possession. "Someone stole their suitcases."
> *They're* is a contraction. It ties together *they* and *are.* "They're a wonderful couple."

Its/It's. Correct use of these is important, too.

> *Its* involves possession. "The fox returned to its lair."
> *It's* is a contraction. It ties together *it* and *is.* "It's my birthday."

Note that *its* is an exception to the usual possessive, in which possession is indicated with *'s*—as in "Bill's new car is a Porsche."

Who's/Whose. Correct use of these avoids confusion.

> *Whose* involves possession. "Whose book is this?"
> *Who's* is a contraction. It ties together *who* and *is.* "Who's coming to your party?"

Faulty Pronoun Reference. A pronoun is a word used in place of a noun or another pronoun that precedes it (an antecedent). There are two rules to remember about using pronouns:

> Pronouns must agree with antecedents in number (singular or plural). "Everyone should put his (or her) coat away." (Note that *everyone* is singular, and so requires a singular pronoun—*his* or *her*—and not a plural—*their.*)
> Pronouns refer to nouns or pronouns that immediately precede them. Here's an example of faulty pronoun usage: "Clutching his fried chicken, John got in his car and started eating it." The *it* here refers to the car, not the chicken. This sentence should be changed to something like "John got in his car and started eating fried chicken."

Pronoun usage is important in scriptwriting because if you make a mistake with your pronouns in your script, both the performers and your listeners will get confused. Always be careful when you use *it*!

Faulty Verb Agreement. Verbs must agree with their subjects. Otherwise, people get confused. If a subject is single, it takes a singular verb. For example: "John [single subject] loves [singular form of verb] ice cream.

If John and Bill feel the same way about ice cream, the verb form changes, because John and Bill take a plural verb: "John and Bill [plural] love [plural form of verb] ice cream."

If you are unsure, ask yourself whether you can say *they* for some construction; if you can, it is plural and takes a plural verb form. Here is the way the verb *to love* is conjugated:

I love ice cream.
You love ice cream.
He/she/it loves ice cream.
We love ice cream.
You (plural) love ice cream.
They love ice cream.

Faulty Punctuation. This is another major problem for scriptwriters. Think of punctuation as being the equivalent to red lights and stop signs on the highway. If people don't know when to stop or when to start, they become confused. The same thing applies to punctuation. *You should always read your scripts out loud*—this will often alert you to punctuation problems in your script.

Here are a few principles to keep in mind when using punctuation.

Commas are used to indicate brief pauses and to separate elements in a sentence or speech.
Semicolons indicate slightly longer pauses than commas.
Colons are used for much longer pauses—to introduce lists and the like.
Dashes (which are typed using two hyphens with no space between them) are used for long pauses—to indicate something important is coming up or to suggest some kind of a change in thought or tone.
Hyphens are used to make compound words or to connect two words, as in *French-American*.
Three dots (ellipses) are also used to indicate a pause, of indeterminate length. This pause is longer than that indicated by a comma or a semicolon and cannot be used to substitute for them, but it can be used, at times, to substitute for a dash.

Punctuation is important because it affects how performers say their lines. Different punctuation marks suggest pauses of different lengths. This means a line that is improperly punctuated can easily be ruined.

Padding, Wordy Writing. Writing that has been padded might use 25 words to say what can be said in 5 words, or repeats itself, saying the same thing two different ways. Students writing term papers often pad because they don't have enough ideas and have to write a certain number of words. For example:

Padding: I would like to state that I believe . . .
Corrected: I think . . .

If you have a character who you want to come across as voluble or a pedant or something like that, then it makes sense to give him or her lines that are wordy. Otherwise, avoid padding.

Incoherent Writing. This refers to writing that doesn't flow, that jumps around and leaves readers or listeners confused. One way to write dialogue that is coherent is to use transitions, which guide the reader or listener along. Transitions tell us what to expect. If we hear, for example, a character say "On the one hand" about a situation, we can expect to hear also "on the other hand," which will tell us something about the other side of the situation.

Primer-style writing, which was discussed in Chapter 1, is also often incoherent. Primer-style dialogue is constructed of very short, very simple sentences—the kind found in storybooks written for young children. This kind of writing is generally inappropriate in works for adults.

Unclear Writing. Unclear writing is hard to understand; it is confusing and ambiguous, at best, and sometimes unintelligible. Usually writing is unclear because it contains a number of grammatical errors and language is not used properly, or because the writer hasn't thought things through and decided what to say. When the writing is substandard and does not follow the rules and conventions of English grammar, you find things like run-on sentences, faulty verb agreement, faulty pronoun references, shifts in person and number, and misplaced modifiers.

Writing should always be clear and intelligible. What happens, in some cases, is that writers forget that they have stored material in their heads that might make a passage clear. They know what they meant to write, but what they put down confuses the reader or listener, who does not have access to this "hidden" information. In other cases, writers have not learned grammar and cannot write acceptable English.

Awkward Writing. This refers to writing that is stiff and ungainly. Usually this is because the writer's sentence construction and language usage are poor. Such a writer lacks grace (like a dancer who knows the steps for a dance but doesn't execute them very well).

In some cases, awkward writing results from inadvertent repetition of a sentence structure ("I believe" followed by "I think" followed by "I want to say"). We find this kind of repetition in cases where a writer has learned only one way to construct a sentence: subject, verb, and object, which is then repeated over and over again.

Reading a script out loud is a good way to find awkward passages. It is also helpful to read a script into a tape recorder and listen to it with a critical ear. Look for dialogue that is hard to follow, that doesn't sound good. The best way to deal with unclear and awkward dialogue is to write new material, rather than try to fix something that is severely flawed.

Undeveloped Writing. Undeveloped writing lacks detail; it tends to be vague and abstract, operating at a high level of generality. It frequently skips from one point to another, with little detail in between. It often reads like an outline that is not fleshed out with examples. Undeveloped writing generally lacks concepts (that help us organize ideas) and color (to make the material engaging).

Here are some approaches you can use in your writing to make it more appealing to readers and listeners:

(1) *Contrast and comparison.* Comparisons and contrasts can help us get a sense of what something is like. "Americans are X but the French are Y," we might say, or "He looks something like Arnold Schwarzenegger." Comparison and contrast help put flesh on the bones of dialogue.

(2) *Definitions.* Defining what we mean by a certain term or giving our understanding of it helps people get a better picture of things, because they know how we are using the term. In some cases where there are numerous definitions, some of which conflict (as with the term *violence*, for example), it is necessary to explain how you are using a term.

(3) *Cause and effect.* This is a means of explaining things for people—we suggest what it is that (in our opinion) brought a certain event or situation about. Of course, just because something (Johnny watches *Batman* on TV) comes before something else (Johnny jumps out of the window) doesn't mean the first thing caused the second. But we all want to know why things happen, and cause and effect is a good way to inject interest and detail into writing.

(4) *Examples.* We can look upon examples as "case histories." As such, they are one of the best ways to generate interest and involvement in readers and listeners. Examples enable us to move from the general or abstract (ideas, concepts, principles, abstractions) to the particular (this happened, that happened).

Trite Expressions and Clichés. "Last, but not least," let me end this chapter with a brief discussion of triteness and clichés. You should avoid this material, as they say, "like the plague." Trite expressions and clichés, like the ones I've just used, are shopworn phrases that people sometimes use because they are convenient and easily understandable. But they are boring and overused, and you should find other ways of expressing yourself when possible. Sometimes, of course, they express an idea perfectly and can't be avoided, but most of the time you should keep away from clichés and trite expressions.

Final Thoughts

I have dealt above with some of the most common errors people make when they write, but I can alert you only to some of the "worst offenders." Every writer should have, as a minimum, a good dictionary, a thesaurus, and a grammar book—and should make good use of them. We all forget, from time to time, the various rules of grammar or how to spell a word. That's natural. But when we write a script, we have an obligation to our audiences to write correctly. That's the least we can do.

If you use a word processor, I would suggest you print out your first draft and make your revisions on the printout. Somehow, making revisions at the keyboard on the screen just doesn't work very well. And if you revise your script three or four times, which Woody Allen and countless other writers tell us is necessary, you'll avoid a lot of eyestrain, too.

... and Ronda with the old windows of the posadas glancing eyes a lattice hid for her lover to kiss the iron and the wineshops half open at night and the castanets and the night we missed the boat at Algeciras the watchman going about serene with his lamp and O that awful deepdown torrent O and the sea the sea crimson sometimes like fire and the glorious sunsets and the figtrees in the Alameda gardens yes and all the queer little streets and pink and blue and yellow houses and the rosegardens and the jessamine and geraniums and cactuses and Gibraltar as a girl where I was a Flower of the mountain yes when I put the rose in my hair like the Andalusian girls used or shall I wear a red yes and how he kissed me under the Moorish wall and I thought well as well him as another and then I asked him with my eyes to ask again yes and then he asked me would I yes to say yes my mountain flower and first I put my arms around him yes and drew him down to me so he could feel my breasts all perfume yes and his heart was going like mad and yes I said yes I will Yes.

—James Joyce, *Ulysses* (1934, pp. 767-768)

15

Teaching Suggestions: A Note to Writing Teachers (But Students, You May Read This If You Want To)

In this chapter I will describe how I use this book when I teach writing for radio and television. There are all kinds of different courses in broadcast writing, due to everything from the size of the department to the particular interests of instructors. But there is only a limited number of kinds of scripts that students have to know about, and this book covers them.

I happen to teach in a rather large department and we have a general course on writing, which most students take, as well as separate courses on writing news and dramatic writing. Because many general broadcast writing courses deal with news and dramatic writing, I've included chapters on these topics. We meet in three-hour class periods once a week, and this has an impact on the way the class is taught. I like the three-hour period very much. In the first part of the period I have students "produce" (act out) their scripts and then, afterward, do peer evaluations. In the second segment, we discuss things, see television programs and films related to our interests, or do group writing exercises.

Scripts "Produced" in Class

I have students "produce" their scripts in class. That is, I ask them to select classmates to read the various parts in the scripts.

173

I find this to be very useful. Students get to see how other students have dealt with assignments, and having an audience tends to stimulate them. For television scripts, I ask the writer to read the video section, at the appropriate times, so we can visualize the shots that would be used with segments of the dialogue. As the semester progresses, I notice that the quality of the acting gets better and better, and many of these little ad hoc productions are quite fine.

Peer Evaluations

After the scripts are read, I pair the students off and ask them to spend about 10 minutes doing peer evaluations of one another's work. I have a form that I ask each evaluator to fill out (see Exhibit 15.1), which is given to the author of the script being evaluated. I also have students bring two copies of all scripts to class—one for me and one for the peer evaluator. I ask the students to write scripts in terms of word counts, not time. I find that assigning a 30-second script is too vague and leads to scripts of widely varying lengths. I tend to approximate what is found on the broadcast media, but often assign longer scripts so the students will have more of an opportunity to develop their ideas.

It is important, I believe, to emphasize to the students that they should be as imaginative as they can. For instance, when we are doing commercials, I ask them to think of me as a "good client" who is open to creativity and risk taking. Those who will go on to work in advertising may not have much freedom in the so-called real world, but in class I think we should stress being inventive. I also stress that the students must be extremely careful about what they write and make sure they do not (even inadvertently) insult any racial, sexual, religious, ethnic, or other group.

Group Writing Exercises

One teaching technique that I've found to be extremely effective involves group writing exercises. I break my class into

Exhibit 15.1: Sample Peer Evaluation Form

Date: _____ Assignment: _____
Evaluator's Name: _____
Writer's Name: _____

1. Read the paper and indicate to what degree has writer followed the specifications for the assignment.

2. What do you feel are the strongest/best aspects of the paper? Please be specific. Indicate in margin "very good, etc."

3. What parts of the assignment do you think need to be strengthened? Please be specific. Underline and indicate in margin "needs work, etc." Indicate any of the errors listed below.

   A. *Spelling Errors.* Circle error and write SP.
   B. *Punctuation Errors.* Circle error and fix. Write PUNCT.
   C. *Problems with Clarity.* Put UNCL next to lines that need work.
   D. *Problems with Awkwardness.* Put AWK next to lines that are awkward.
   E. *Poor Word Choice.* Circle word(s) and write WORD CHOICE.
   F. *Wordy Passages.* Underline and write WORDY.
   G. *Trite Passages.* Underline and write TRITE.
   H. *Overly Complex Sentences.* Write TOO COMPLEX.
   I. *Anything Else.*

4. Write a note on the paper describing your assessment of the paper, with specific references to the writer's style, good points, bad points, etc.

groups of three students, have them form their seats into "tri-angles," and ask them to work on various exercises "collec-tively." This group writing has several benefits. First, the students get to know one another and feel less inhibited about contributing to class discussions. Second, the students seem to stimulate one another and "feed off" one another's ideas and imaginations. The level of animation and excitement in these groups is, at times, remarkable. I usually move from group to group and chat with the students about what they are doing and answer any questions they have about the exercises. At the end of the time allotted for group work, I ask the students to read what they have written or, in the case of scripts, "pro-duce" them. The exercises I assign are found at the ends of the various chapters in this book.

Let me offer a couple of examples. When I teach comedy writing, I offer two "one-hour" (approximately) workshops. In the first, we use the Comedy Calculator (see Chapter 3). I explain my theory that all humor is based on the use of tech-niques and show how we can find these techniques in a couple of jokes, which are broken down into techniques in the Comedy Calculator. Then I form the students into groups of three per-sons and ask each group to come to a decision, collectively, about the jokes I have provided in this exercise. That is, they must reduce them all to formulas: one subject and no more than three techniques. This exercise might be looked upon as a parody of social science.

After a half hour, I ask one member of each team to write the formulas for the jokes in a chart I've drawn on the blackboard, so I end up with seven or eight team lists of formulas. Then we see whether the groups agreed on subjects and techniques and discuss the differences we find. The students generally find this exercise quite bizarre, but they come away from it with an understanding of my notion that there are a number of tech-niques that are found in humor. I explain to them that I use jokes in the Comedy Calculator only because they are short and easy to use, and that I suggest they avoid jokes when they want to write in a humorous manner.

The next exercise is also zany, but at the end of it the stu-dents have actually created some good comedy writing and sometimes write some ingenious scripts. This exercise involves playing with the "eye" sound. The sound can come in the middle or at the end of words, with special points for farfetched eye sounds, the use of foreign languages, double eye sounds, and so on. I suggest the students think in terms of riddles about ophthalmologists. For example, Question: "What psychological problems do ophthalmologists have?" Answer: "Anxieties." They then list some 30 or 40 eye sounds and collectively write a script involving ophthalmologists—their loves, adventures, problems, travels, habits, preoccupations, and so on. Some of the stories they write are very amusing.

Another exercise involves writing a simple story in different styles. I read some of Queneau's stylistic variations and then give students the outline of a story very similar to the one he uses. I also give them a list of six or eight styles and ask them to write scripts in any two or three styles. This often produces some really wild and wonderful scripts. Another similar exercise involves retelling a simple story in terms of different genres.

I've also asked students to write two parodies—of catalog course descriptions (of one or two of our required courses) and of my course and style of teaching. I have another exercise that involves having them write "features" based on a newspaper article of interest. When we deal with editorials, I have them write an editorial (unsigned) to the department chair, which I give to him, and to which he invariably responds. These exercises, which require students to write in different styles and different genres, to analyze humor, and to try their hands at writing it (using wordplay and writing parodies), all are very useful, I believe, in enlarging their horizons and sense of possibility.

Keeping Journals

I have the students keep journals. I also ask the students to bring their journals to class, because just about every period I ask them to write in their journals for 5-10 minutes. I usually suggest some topic, which generally has to do with writing, creativity, and related concerns. Students who wish to get full credit for their journals must write five pages per week, including the classroom journal writing. I have them purchase laboratory notebooks that are bound and have numbered pages.

Although students often grumble about keeping journals, I find that by the end of the semester the majority of them feel that the exercise was useful, in that it helped them develop their ideas and got them thinking like writers. I give partial credit for journals that don't have the required number of pages, and I don't give full credit for journals that are full of personal material and have little to do with writing, thinking about and planning writing, ideas, and the like. It is impossible to avoid some personal material in the journals, but their focus should not be on this kind of thing. A certain amount of latitude has to be given on this matter.

I collect the journals a week before the end of classes and read them. Then I give each one a certain number of points, depending on how good the journal is and how much was written. I return the journals the last day of class, when we have a party.

Class Schedule Formats

I have found it useful to offer two formats for the course schedule, one linear and the other in chart form (see the example that follows). The students seem to find the chart format useful in that it organizes each class period in a more visual manner than the linear format, though one can put more material into a linear schedule. Somehow, having two formats seems to help them keep track of things better.

Example of Possible Radio and TV Writing Schedule

1.	2.	3.	4.
Introduction. Course described. In-class writing. Student intros assigned.	Student intros. PSA assigned. Docu topics due, discussed.	PSAs due. Radio commercial assigned. Film on Woody Allen. Docus discussed.	Radio commercials due. Comedy work shop: joke analysis.
5.	6.	7.	8.
Docu forms due. TV commercials assigned. Show George Lois documentary. Comedy workshop.	TV commercials due. Film parodies shown. Parodies assigned.	Parodies due, discussed. Documentaries. Team writing: genres. Dramas assigned.	Dramas due, discussed. Team writing: descriptive writing.

9.	10.	11.	12.
Docu packets due. Film review assigned. Show film for review.	Film reviews due. Show documentary, discuss. Comedy commercial assigned.	Comedy commercial due, discussed. Team writing: styles.	Features due, discussed. Team writing: features.
13.	**14.**	**15.**	
Documentaries due. Show editorials. Team writing: editorials.	Editorials due. Course evaluations. Team writing. News scripts assigned.	News scripts due, discussed. P A R T Y .	

The First Assignment

My first assignment (which is not graded) is to have each student write a two- or three-page radio script, in the proper format, with full production values (a number of characters, sound, music) about him- or herself. This is due at the second class meeting. It is a much better way of getting students to introduce themselves to the members of the class than asking them to tell something about themselves directly.

Each student must pass in a script, but I also allow students to get together with friends and make tapes of their script, with music and sound effects, which we play when we get together for our second class meeting. I then ask the students to speculate in their journals about what they learned from the assignment and why I asked them to write the scripts. We then discuss what they have written in their journals.

The Documentary

I require all students to do a documentary of between 10 and 12 pages. This assignment is described in Chapter 8. I find that this "simulation," using printed matter as the equivalent of taped interviews, works very well—and asking the students to pass in a "documentary packet" does a wonderful job of forcing them to concentrate their minds and organize their research. It is also a good idea to have the students write an 80-word promo for their documentaries. This forces them to give their documentaries a bit of focus.

We discuss the documentary at various times during the semester; I require the students to choose a specific subject, usually by the fifth week of class, and to pass in their documentary packets by the tenth week of class. Then I give them a few weeks to write the script and usually have them pass it in a week before classes end. I need more than a week to grade the scripts, so I ask them to put their scripts in large (9 by 12 inch) self-addressed stamped manila envelopes.

Choice of Exercises

All the students have to do documentaries and the various assignments that are connected with the documentaries, but they have choices concerning all the other scripts. (For example, you might assign 10 different kinds of scripts and ask the students to write any 7 scripts they wish.) Since they are given a considerable amount of choice, I don't accept any late scripts, for any reason.

Giving the students an element of choice reduces the stress level and allows students to choose the kind of writing they find most interesting. I can conceive of a modification on my strategy. That is, students might be required to write one or two other kinds of scripts, in addition to the documentaries. A good deal depends on what you think they should know how to write. If my department had no courses in news writing or dramatic writing, I probably would require students to do a news story and to write a short dramatic script.

I happen to be interested in humor and think that comedy writing is important and is a good way of maintaining student interest, so I assign several different kinds of comedy scripts. But students who find comedy writing difficult or who have other interests can avoid these assignments and focus on other kinds of writing more to their taste.

Use of Media and Speakers

I use a lot of media in the course. I have taped editorials and commercials that are useful for those assignments. There are many tapes available on commercials, advertising, marketing, and related concerns. I also show documentaries and discuss them. One of my colleagues, John Hewitt, has made an excellent documentary, *Tremors in Guznan,* so I usually show it and then have him come in and discuss it with the class.

I show an interesting film for the film review assignment and, from time to time, I bring people in from local advertising agencies and radio and television stations to talk about their work and the importance of writing in the broadcast media. There are also many wonderful television programs that have been made for public television (and commercially made films and documentaries) in which poets and writers are interviewed that can be used.

Teaching Writing Is Fun

I love to teach writing. I often find myself eager to come to class to see what my students have come up with in their scripts. Writing for radio and television is what I would describe as "imaginative" writing. I don't like to use the word *creative* because I think most writing is creative. You don't have to write fiction or poetry to use your imagination and be inventive—and interesting. Actually, writing for radio and television offers students unusual opportunities to be imaginative and inventive (which is what we usually mean by *creative*), and this volume, I'd like to think, has been designed to exploit these opportunities in positive ways.

Writing is that "play" by which I turn around as well as I can in a narrow place. I am wedged in. I struggle between the hysteria necessary to write and the image-repertoire, which oversees, controls, purifies, banalizes, codifies, corrects, and imposes the focus (and the vision) of a social communication. On the one hand I want to be desired and on the other not to be desired: hysterical and obsessional at one and the same time. . . .

And afterward?
—What to write now? Can you still write anything?
—One writes with one's desire, and I am not through desiring.

—Roland Barthes, *Roland Barthes* (1977, p. 137)

Epilogue

Benjamin Franklin, in many ways the archetypal American, the original "self-made man," has something interesting to say about writing in his autobiography: "but as prose writing has been of great use to me in the course of my life, and was a principal means of my advancement, I shall tell you how, in such a situation, I acquired what little ability I have in that way." He mentions that his father read some of his writings and pointed out certain weaknesses in them. Franklin continues: "I saw the justice of his remarks, and thence grew more attentive to the *manner* of writing, and determined to endeavor at improvement."

He discovered, among other things, that his vocabulary was limited and that he wrote in a confusing manner. (In short, Benjamin Franklin, were he alive now, would almost certainly have been required to take a course in freshman English.) He mastered these skills on his own and went on, as anyone familiar with early American history knows, to have a really wild time in France (the first of the expatriate writers?) and "to dine with kings."

Writing is a means of advancement for many people. I know people who seem to have satisfying lives and have a wonderful time as copywriters, novelists, screenplay writers, teleplay writers, journalists, writers of scholarly books, and even textbook writers. When I was young I liked to write—but the notion that I could ever write a book never dawned on me. It was something strange people called "writers" did—God knows how. In college, a 10-page term paper seemed pretty awesome. How in the hell does anyone write 200 pages or 500 pages? The answer, of course, is a word at a time.

I would imagine that were Benjamin Franklin alive now, he would be writing screenplays and teleplays—for it is writing, along with sales, that is probably the best way to get into the filmmaking, radio, and television industries. If that's what you want—and the fact that you are reading this book suggests you have taken a radio and television writing course and have an interest in broadcasting—what are you waiting for? Get that journal out and start writing.

You may not get to dine with kings; your involvement with royalties may be of a different nature—that is, a great big check in the mail. That can be very pleasant, too (so I've heard).

Bibliography

Adams, H. (1931). *The education of Henry Adams.* New York: Random House.

Allen, W. (Ed.). (1959). *Writers on writing.* New York: Dutton.

Barthes, R. (1977). *Roland Barthes.* New York: Hill & Wang.

Beckett, S. (1960). *Krapp's last tape.* New York: Grove.

Berger, A. A. (1976). Anatomy of the joke. *Journal of Communication, 26*(3), 113-115.

Berger, A. A. (1982). *Media analysis techniques.* Beverly Hills, CA: Sage.

Berger, A. A. (1984). *Signs in contemporary culture: An introduction to semiotics.* New York: Longman.

Berne, E. (1964). *Games people play: The psychology of human relationships.* New York: Grove.

Brady, J. (Ed.). (1981). *The craft of the screenwriter: Interviews with six celebrated screenwriters.* New York: Simon & Schuster.

Cantril, H. (1940). *Invasion from Mars: A study in the psychology of panic.* Princeton, NJ: Princeton University Press.

Edmonds, R. (1974). *About documentary: Anthropology on film.* Dayton, OH: Pflaum.

Elliot, B., & Goulding, R. (1985). *From approximately coast to coast . . . It's the Bob and Ray Show.* New York: Penguin.

Epstein, E. J. (1974). *News from nowhere.* New York: Vintage.

Freud, S. (1963). *Jokes and their relation to the unconscious.* New York: W. W. Norton.

Gado, F. (Ed.). (1973). *First person: Conversations on writers and writing.* Schenectady, NY: Union College Press.

Gardner, J. (1983). *On becoming a novelist.* New York: Harper & Row.

Garvey, D. E., & Rivers, W. L. (1982). *Broadcast writing.* New York: Longman.

Gitlin, T. (1987). Television's screens: Hegemony in transition. In D. Lazere (Ed.), *Media and mass culture.* Berkeley: University of California Press.

Hemingway, E. (1983). *To have and have not.* New York: Scribner.

Hewitt, J. (1988). *Air words: Writing for broadcast news.* Mountain View, CA: Mayfield.

Hildrick, W. (1970). *Thirteen types of narrative.* New York: Clarkson N. Potter.

Ionesco, E. (1958). *Four plays.* New York: Grove.

Joyce, J. (1934). *Ulysses.* New York: Random House.

Kavan, A. (1973). *Ice.* London: Picador.

Lakoff, G., & Johnson, M. (1980). *Metaphors we live by.* Chicago: University of Chicago Press.

Lowery, S., & de Fleur, M. (1983). *Milestones in mass communication research: Media effects.* New York: Longman.

Maloney, M., & Rubenstein, P. M. (1980). *Writing for the media.* Englewood Cliffs, NJ: Prentice-Hall.

Mayeux, P. F. (1985). *Writing for the broadcast media.* Boston: Allyn & Bacon.

Monaco, J. (1977). *How to read a film.* New York: Oxford University Press.

Murray, D. M. (1985). *A writer teaches writing* (2nd ed.). Boston: Houghton Mifflin.

Orlik, P. B. (1982). *Broadcast copywriting* (2nd ed.). Boston: Allyn & Bacon.

Pirandello, L. (1952). *Naked masks: Five plays by Luigi Pirandello.* New York: Dutton.

Queneau, R. (1981). *Exercises in style* (B. Wright, Trans.). New York: New Directions.

Rivers, W. L. (1975). *Writing: Craft and art.* Englewood Cliffs, NJ: Prentice-Hall.

Simon, N. (1973). *The comedy of Neil Simon.* New York: Avon.

Stoppard, T. (1975). *Travesties.* New York: Evergreen.

Trimble, J. R. (1975). *Writing with style.* Englewood Cliffs, NJ: Prentice-Hall.

Welty, E. (1984). *One writer's beginnings.* Cambridge, MA: Harvard University Press.

West, N. (1959). *Miss Lonelyhearts.* New York: Avon.

Zinsser, W. (1985). *On writing well: An informal guide to writing nonfiction.* New York: Harper & Row.

Name Index

Subject Index

About the Author

Arthur Asa Berger is Professor of Broadcast Communication Arts at San Francisco State University, where he has taught since 1965. He has written extensively on popular culture, the mass media, and related concerns. Among his books are *Media Analysis Techniques* (Sage Publications), *Agitpop: Political Culture and Communication Theory* (Transaction Books), *Seeing Is Believing* (Mayfield Publishing), and *Media USA* (Longman, Inc.). *Scripts* is his seventeenth book and his second book for Sage Publications.

Dr. Berger had a Fulbright to Italy in 1963 and taught at the University of Milan. He has lectured extensively on media and popular culture—in Denmark, Norway, Sweden, and Finland as a guest of the Nordic Institute of Folklore; in Greece, Lebanon, and Turkey in 1973 and in Brazil in 1987 for the United States Information Agency; and in Germany, France, the People's Republic of China, and England at the request of various universities and institutions. He is a Consulting and Contributing Editor for the *Journal of Communications,* Film and Television Review Editor for *Society* magazine, editor of a series of reprints, "Classics in Communications" for Transaction Books, and a consulting editor for *Humor* magazine. He has appeared on *20/20* and the *Today* show, and appears frequently on various local television and radio stations in the San Francisco area.

He is married to Phyllis Wolfson Berger, who teaches philosophy at Diablo Valley College, and has a daughter, Miriam Beesley, who is a scriptwriter, and a son, Gabriel Berger, who is working on a Ph.D. in mathematics at Columbia University.

NOTES